Latimer Studies 88

Focus on Jesus

A Guide to the Message of Handel's *Messiah*

Robert Bashford

The Latimer Trust

ISBN 978-1-906327-61-3

Cover photo: 'Empty Tomb' by Kevin Carden on Adobe Stock.

Published by the Latimer Trust June 2020.

The Latimer Trust (formerly Latimer House, Oxford) is a conservative Evangelical research organisation within the Church of England, whose main aim is to promote the history and theology of Anglicanism as understood by those in the Reformed tradition. Interested readers are welcome to consult its website for further details of its many activities.

The Latimer Trust

London N14 4PS UK

Registered Charity: 1084337

Company Number: 4104465

Web: www.latimertrust.org

E-mail: administrator@latimertrust.org

Copyright information

Acknowledgements and general comments

Appreciation is expressed to many Bible teachers whose helpful insights have been invaluable in commenting on the Bible passages that are used in *Messiah* and to friends whose comments about plans for this book have been appreciated. Various articles on Handel's *Messiah* have been a useful source in preparation for this book.

The following abbreviations are used:

AV = Authorised Version (1611) – otherwise known as the King James' Version

RV = Revised Version (1881)

NIV = New International Version (1978)

ESV = English Standard Version (2011 Revision)

Bible quotations are from the ESV, unless otherwise indicated.

Contents

Introduction

Part I: From Heaven to Earth

Part II: From the Cross to Glory

Part III: From Death to Life

Introduction

The aim of this book

At the risk of making an obvious comment, Handel's oratorio *Messiah* is amazingly Christ-centred from beginning to end. All who listen to a performance of the work are drawn to focus on Jesus and to consider who he is and what he has done. While we are rightly moved by the superb music of *Messiah* – which ranges from rousing, exciting sections to passages of intense poignancy – we are also brought face to face with the Lord Jesus Christ through the Bible texts selected to be sung by the soloists and chorus. It is well worth taking time to examine the oratorio's portrayal of Jesus, and that is what we shall do in these pages.

This book is aimed at a wide readership. There is no expectation that anyone picking up this book should be an expert in Handel or music or theology. Even without a guide to Handel's *Messiah,* a performance of the oratorio makes a powerful impact on most listeners. But this book may help to draw attention to aspects of the work which have not been noticed before or to reinforce those that have.

Most of this book will consist of comments on the Bible texts, in order to explain their meaning both in their original Bible context and in their contribution to the oratorio's presentation of Jesus. A number of illustrations are included along the way, in much the same way as will happen in many a sermon. Several of these come from the writings of C S Lewis, whose insights can be so instructive. The hope is that this additional material will help to engage the attention of readers rather than proving to be a distraction.

Comments on the Bible texts are interspersed with shorter sections about the music of *Messiah,* with the heading 'What to listen out for in the music'. These sections are printed on a darker background, so that readers can easily choose between sections on the text or on the music. An awareness of certain features of the music can contribute to our enjoyment of the work and at the same time enhance our understanding of the message of *Messiah.* Readers will come to this book with a wide variety of musical backgrounds, so the aim is to strike a balance somewhere between too much and too little explanation of musical terms.

One of the recurring themes In Handel's *Messiah* is that Jesus is the 'light of the world'. His entry into this world means that 'the people who walked in darkness have seen a great light; those who dwelt in a land of deep darkness, on them has light shined' (Isa 9:2 – one of the work's Bible texts, quoted in part I of the oratorio). How marvellous it would be if all who read this book have, as a result, a deeper experience of the great joy of living in the light of the Messiah.

Who is the Messiah?

The Messiah is, of course, the Lord Jesus Christ. But we also need to be aware of the Old Testament's anticipation of his coming. The word 'Messiah' means 'the anointed one' and comes from a Hebrew root, being the equivalent of the word 'Christ' which comes from the Greek. In Old Testament times, kings in particular were anointed, as in the case of Saul or David (1 Samuel 10:1, 16:13).[1] Being anointed signified being set apart for God and it carried authority. Throughout the Old Testament, the expectation grew that God would send a particular individual as his 'anointed' who would be the ideal king.

As is only to be expected, a good number of the Bible's references to the Messiah appear in this oratorio. But a brief focus now on five key Old Testament passages which look forward to the Messiah's arrival will help to set the scene – and these important passages will be referred to from time to time in this book, some more than others:

- Genesis 3:15 contains what should be seen as the first Bible reference to the expectation of the Christ, even though there is no mention of the term Messiah or king. Following Adam and Eve's act of disobedience to God (the event known as the Fall), God's curse on the serpent includes the promise of a deliverer to come. God says to the serpent, 'I will put enmity between you and the woman, and between your offspring and her offspring; he shall bruise your head, and you shall bruise his heel.' The woman's 'offspring' (or 'seed') will defeat the

[1] Priests were also anointed (Ex.28:41) and also prophets (1 Kings 19:16).

serpent ('he shall bruise your head'), although at cost to himself ('you shall bruise his heel').

- Genesis 12:1–3 is a particularly important passage with messianic implications. In these verses God makes three promises to Abraham: a) to give him a land, b) to make of him a great nation, c) to make him and his posterity a blessing to 'all the families of the earth'.[2] According to the New Testament, this amazing promise is fulfilled in Jesus Christ.[3]

- Genesis 49:10, part of Jacob's blessings on his sons, is the first 'royal' reference to the expected Messiah: 'The sceptre shall not depart from Judah'. Centuries later, when David (from the tribe of Judah) was anointed king, this Biblical prophecy (as we must surely describe it) would have taken on fresh significance.

- 2 Samuel 7:12–14 records words which were originally addressed to King David by the prophet Nathan, when God promised that David's house (or dynasty) would last 'for ever'. This promise should be seen as pointing forward to Jesus, 'great David's greater Son', the Messiah–King and the eternal Son.[4]

- Psalm 2 expresses the hope of a messianic king particularly clearly. 'The Lord' and 'his Anointed' are linked together in verse 2. In verse 6, God announces, 'As for me, I have set my King on Zion, my holy hill.' Then, in verse 7, in words which are put on the lips of the Christ (the Lord's 'Anointed'), we read, 'I will tell of the decree: The Lord said to me, "You are my Son; today I have begotten you."'

All these promises and expectations, and so many others as well, find their fulfilment in the coming of Jesus. Peter's identification of Jesus as

---

[2] His name was still Abram at this time and was changed to Abraham in Genesis 17:5.

[3] In particular, see Galatians 3:7-9, 16, 29.

[4] From James Montgomery's hymn, *Hail To The Lord's Anointed* – a hymn worth reading through, as it encapsulates much of the Old Testament's expectation of the Messiah, fulfilled in Jesus.

the Christ (or the Messiah), on behalf of all the disciples, marks a significant moment in Jesus' ministry (Matt 16:16, Mark 8:29, Luke 9:20).

The background to *Messiah*

It may come as a surprise to realise that we owe this oratorio to *two* men, not just its composer, George Frideric Handel. We must also recognise the amazing contribution of Charles Jennens, who was responsible for compiling the Bible texts used in the oratorio. Both men deserve to be introduced briefly.

Handel the composer

George Frideric Handel was born in Halle (Germany) in 1685. He gave evidence of great musical ability from an early age. His father had plans for the young Handel to enter the legal profession but he gave up his legal studies in favour of a career in music and began to gain a considerable reputation as a composer. A visit to Italy was a major influence on his style of musical composition. In his 20s, he settled in London during the reign of Queen Anne, at a time when Italian music was becoming fashionable. England remained Handel's home from that time onwards.

Like all court composers of his age, he provided whatever his patrons required – whether chamber music or church music. His work included fine pieces as the *Water Music*, the *Royal Fireworks Music* and four anthems written for the coronation of George II in 1727. One of them, *Zadok the Priest*, has been performed at every English coronation since then.

But Handel's heart was set on music for the theatre and he wrote a number of Italian-texted operas. Despite his initial success in this genre, the popularity of Italian opera declined and, during the 1730s, Handel began to turn his attention to English-texted oratorios on religious topics. Meanwhile, he also continued to devote his energies to opera, but dwindling audiences gave rise to severe financial difficulties. His last opera *Deidamia*, written in 1741, was such a disaster that he was finally forced to abandon opera altogether. This period of time marked a low point in Handel's career: besides his money worries, he was overworked and deeply depressed by the failure of his operatic ventures. But it was during this crisis, in July 1741, that Handel received the text of *Messiah* from Charles Jennens, a wealthy industrialist and patron of the arts.

Jennens the librettist

'Libretto' is the technical term used for the literary text of an opera or oratorio, so 'librettist' is the word for the person responsible for this work. Charles Jennens does not receive the recognition he deserves. His name is hardly known, even by many who are familiar with his enduring legacy in the libretto of *Messiah.* While musicologists are divided in their assessment of Jennens in general terms, one of them writes that the text for *Messiah* 'amounts to little short of a work of genius.'[5] Jennens was a good friend to Handel over a long period of time. He had provided Handel with the texts for earlier oratorios in the 1730s. He had also helped to finance the publication of every Handel score since the mid-1720s. Undoubtedly, a warm friendship had developed between the two men by 1741.

Jennens was a devout Anglican and firmly believed in scriptural authority. It seems that part of Jennens's purpose in compiling the libretto for *Messiah* was to challenge the then prevalent deist view which regarded God as distant and uninvolved in human affairs. What better way of showing the error of such thinking than to focus on the entry into the world of God's promised Messiah; his amazing act of involving himself in the predicament of a fallen human race by taking their sins upon himself on the cross; and his triumphant rule over the nations of the world!

The composition of Messiah

Handel was struck immediately by the possibilities of the text and he began work in a truly inspired manner. He composed the entire oratorio in a breathtaking 24 days (22 August to 14 September 1741). While he based a few of the choruses on themes borrowed from earlier compositions, this work was nevertheless an outstanding masterpiece. During the time of composition, Handel was totally absorbed in his task and never left the house at all. His servant brought him food but it was often untouched when he returned to collect the dish. At the end of his

[5] H. Watkins Shaw, *The Story of Handel's 'Messiah'* (London: Novello, 1963), 11.

manuscript, Handel wrote the letters 'SDG' – *Soli Deo Gloria* ('To God alone be the glory!').

Initial opposition but growing popularity

Messiah was given its première in Dublin on 13 April 1742. The first performance was warmly received. However, Handel faced opposition from certain quarters. When he had tried to recruit a choir for performances of some of his new works in Dublin, Jonathan Swift (of *Gulliver's Travels* fame and Dean of St Patrick's Cathedral) expressed strong disapproval of cathedral choir members taking part in what he regarded as 'a club of fiddlers'. However, before long, Swift backed down from his opposition to *Messiah* in view of the aim to raise money for a number of good causes in Dublin from performances.

When *Messiah* was performed in London at the Covent Garden theatre on 23 March 1743, it met with a cool reception as it sparked off a controversy about the propriety of religious works being performed in a theatre. It was also felt by some to be inappropriate for sacred texts to be sung in what appeared to be an opera disguised as a concert. For years, the religious controversy kept many people away. Clergy called the oratorio sacrilege and regarded Handel as a heretic.

Gradually, the oratorio weathered the storm and gained respectability. One important step in this direction was achieved by a performance at the Foundling Hospital Chapel in May 1750. The purpose of the Foundling Hospital was the 'Maintenance and Education of Exposed and Deserted Young Children' but it was desperately short of funds in the mid-eighteenth century. As in Dublin eight years earlier, the charitable aim of this performance did much to allay criticism about a work which combined a religious text with theatrical arias. Regular performances continued at the Foundling Hospital into the 1760s – and soon the oratorio was being performed in such places as Derby, Liverpool and Newcastle. In 1757, it was performed for the first time at the Three Choirs' Festival, which rotated annually between the cathedrals of Gloucester, Worcester and Hereford.

Following Handel's death in April 1759, a major step forward in *Messiah*'s popularity came with the two performances at the 1784 Commemoration of Handel in Westminster Abbey. The event was intended to commemorate and celebrate the twenty-fifth anniversary of the composer's death and also the centenary of his birth. The first of these two anniversaries was indeed correct but the second was a miscalculation, as Handel was born in 1685 (not 1684). The error came about as a result of the change in England in 1752 from the Julian calendar (Old Style) to the Gregorian calendar (New Style). The inscription on Handel's tomb in Westminster Abbey makes the same mistake concerning the date of his birth.

The significance of the 1784 Handel Commemoration is that *Messiah* had clearly been fully accepted into English society – and at the highest level, as these concerts were attended by the royal family and were financially underwritten by members of both political parties of the time (Tories and Whigs). Significant too was the number of the performers: about 500 in all.

Since then, Handel's *Messiah* has continued to grow in popularity and must rank as a firm favourite in the repertoire of classical music. As an indicator of its enduring place in popular listening, it has consistently been ranked at about twentieth place in the Classic FM Hall of Fame for most years in the last decade.

How should we approach listening to *Messiah*?

There are a number of things about Handel's *Messiah* which those who are familiar with the work may take for granted, but which those who do not know it so well may find helpful to have explained. Here are some particular features that we need to be aware of.

The 'drama' of the work

An 'oratorio', such as Handel's *Messiah,* is a concert setting of a religious theme of a dramatic nature. It could almost be described as an opera without scenery or costume or action. As mentioned earlier, Handel had composed a number of operas before he turned his attention to oratorios, and features of opera certainly reappear in his oratorios. As noted, this very fact was initially an obstacle to the acceptance of the work.

Musical scores of *Messiah* and most programme notes at concerts make it clear that the oratorio consists of three parts. Those three parts correspond to the normal division of an opera into three acts.

Part I deals with the Old Testament expectation of the Messiah, followed by the angel's announcement to the shepherds of Jesus' birth and, briefly, Jesus' ministry.

Part II begins with the sufferings of Jesus and his death and moves on to his resurrection, ascension and the preaching of the gospel to the nations – 'good tidings' to many, but also opposed by others. It concludes with the triumphant 'Hallelujah' Chorus.

Part III focuses on the 'last things', in particular issues concerning death and resurrection, finishing with words of praise proclaiming, 'Worthy is the Lamb that was slain', followed by the magnificent 'Amen' chorus.

What is not so clear to audiences today is that Jennens arranged his compilation in 'scenes' (16 in total). In doing this, he established a logical sequence in his choice of Bible verses for the libretto for each item within the oratorio.

Having described the oratorio as consisting of three 'parts' (corresponding to acts), and each one divided into a number of 'scenes', a word is needed to describe the individual items of the oratorio. Some of these are solo pieces, and others designed for the chorus. The best word is 'movements' (to borrow a term from the building blocks of orchestral symphonies and concertos).

Jennens provided titles for the scenes but they are never – or certainly very rarely – reproduced in scores or programme notes nowadays. The reason is almost certainly the somewhat wordy nature of his original titles for the parts and the scenes, as may be seen in Appendix 1. This book follows the division of *Messiah* into scenes as Jennens intended, but uses my own simplified, and hopefully more punchy, titles for the three parts and the 16 scenes, as listed on the Contents page.

Anyone listening to a performance or a recording of *Messiah* will not necessarily notice the transition from one scene to the next, but an awareness of the shape of the work definitely adds to its appreciation and, of course, reminds us of the dramatic nature of the work.

The language of the work

The text is based for the most part on the Authorised Version of the Bible (AV), published in 1611 (known also as the King James Version of the

Bible). The antiquated language may be a problem for some today, but readers of a certain age will have been brought up on the Authorised Version in their childhood, and many today still use it for preference. It goes without saying that this was the standard version of the Bible in use in the 1700s and for long afterwards.

Jennens diverges slightly from the AV in two particular ways. First, in the Bible texts from the Psalms, he almost always quotes from the *Book of Common Prayer*, which would have been very familiar to earlier Anglican audiences. Secondly, deliberate minor changes are made to the text of the AV where Bible verses express the actual words of Christ – or, in the case of Old Testament verses, words which could be interpreted as spoken by Christ.[6] With these verses, the first person singular ('I', 'me') is changed to the third person singular ('he', 'him'). One clear example of this is the well-known Movement 20, where the words sung are 'Come unto him' in place of the actual words 'Come unto me' in the Authorised Version of Matthew 11:28. Such changes were made in order to show a degree of reverence and would have forestalled the accusation that a performer was acting the part of Christ.

The large amount of Old Testament material

Jennens makes extensive use of Old Testament verses (not least, Psalms and Isaiah). This happens not only in parts which deal with the Old Testament expectation of the Messiah but also when dealing with the ministry, passion, death, resurrection and ascension of Christ and also the proclamation of the gospel. By contrast, the only verses in the whole oratorio drawn from the Gospels concern:

- the fulfilment of Isaiah's prophecy of Jesus' virgin conception (Matt 1:23)
- the angel's announcement of Christ's birth to the shepherds (Luke 2:8–11, 13–14)
- Jesus' invitation to come to him (Matt 11:28–30)
- John the Baptist's identification of Jesus as 'the Lamb of God' (John 1:29)

[6] Many, but not all, of these minor changes will be noted in the following pages.

Jennens's grasp of the unity of the whole of Scripture, with that unity shaped by the theme of the Messiah, should impress us.

There is nothing remarkable, of course, in going to the Old Testament to find passages anticipating Christ. Jesus himself taught that this is the right approach to Old Testament Scripture. On one occasion he said, 'You search the Scriptures because you think that in them you have eternal life; and it is they that bear witness about me' (John 5:39). He taught the same truth twice following his resurrection in Luke 24. The first time was in his meeting with the two disciples on the Emmaus Road, when Luke tells us: 'And beginning with Moses and all the Prophets, he interpreted to them in all the Scriptures the things concerning himself' (Luke 24:27). The other time was on the evening of the same day, when he spoke to the disciples in the upper room and said, 'everything written about me in the Law of Moses and the Prophets and the Psalms must be fulfilled' (Luke 24:44). What is remarkable about Jennens's approach is that the amount of material he selects from the Old Testament far outweighs material from the New Testament and particularly from the Gospels.

Missing Bible verses

Something that came as a surprise to me in writing this book is Charles Jennens's practice of omitting occasional Bible verses. This may also come as a surprise to others who listen to *Messiah.*

I do not mean by this the absence of Bible verses or passages that we might have chosen to include in our list of what may be called 'messianic material'. When we reflect on what was established in the previous section, namely that all Scripture points to Jesus, that list would surely include the whole Bible! So it would be extremely unfair to criticise Jennens for being selective about which parts of the Bible to include and which parts to exclude.

What I have in mind is that, on a number of occasions, when Jennens has chosen a sequence of verses from the same passage of Scripture (either in the same movement or in consecutive movements), he leaves out a half-verse or a whole verse or even a few verses. The listener may well assume that the sequence of Bible verses is being delivered in its entirety, when that is not the case.

One obvious example appears in the opening movements of the oratorio (Part I Scene 1), where Movements 2–4 appear to be a setting of Isaiah 40:1–5. In fact, the second half of verse 2 of that passage is omitted.

Is this a criticism of Charles Jennens as a librettist? Listeners must make up their own minds on this question. On the one hand, some omissions may be felt to be arbitrary or even disappointing. On the other hand, given that a librettist must be allowed to make editorial decisions, we may well come to the conclusion that there are good reasons for at least some of the omissions. There will be some comment in the following pages on each occurrence of an omission, so that readers can decide on each instance on its own merits.

Regardless of our views on this issue of Bible omissions, Charles Jennens – in my opinion – still deserves to be highly commended for his work in producing the libretto for *Messiah.* His insightful selection and combination of Bible texts, as well as what has been remarked on as his masterly grasp of the Christ-centredness of the whole of Scripture, far outweigh any quibbles we may want to raise with regard to some verses being left to one side.

There is no definitive version of Messiah

This point needs to be made, because the version of the oratorio which you are (or have been) listening to may vary in certain respects from the one that this book comments on.

The oratorio is written for chorus and four solo voices (soprano; contralto, mezzo-soprano or counter-tenor; tenor; and bass). Handel's original orchestra would have consisted of a relatively modest number of strings (violins, violas, cellos and double bass), plus a couple of oboes, a bassoon, two trumpets, timpani, harpsichord and organ. But performances have taken place, and continue to do so, with larger and more extensive combinations of instruments and with more singers in the chorus than originally envisaged. For example, *Messiah* was performed on 15 June 1857 at Crystal Palace, London, when a performance of *Messiah* was given as part of the Great Handel Festival. It included a choir of about 2,000 voices, drawn from amateur musical societies across England, and an orchestra of 300 strings and 90 wind and brass players. Mozart's full-blooded orchestration[7] with extra brass and woodwind is worth listening to for an inspiring experience. By contrast, a relatively small number of musicians – a church choir for example – may perform *Messiah,* or parts of it, accompanied by an organ instead of an orchestra.

The practice of making alterations to *Messiah* goes right back to Handel himself. In the years between the première and his death in 1759, Handel subjected the work to constant revision and modification. Partly this was a matter of replacing a given movement with a preferred version. But other modifications were made to meet the demands (or the inadequacies) of soloists on specific occasions. So while most of the solo items are associated with a particular voice, there is nothing strange about a different voice on occasions singing this or that item.

This paragraph contains somewhat more technical information for those who may find it useful. The numbering of the individual movements in this book is that of the historic Novello edition of 1959, which is based on earlier editions and contains 53 movements. The major alternative numbering system is that of the Bärenreiter edition, edited by John Tobin, published in 1965 in the Hallische Händel-Ausgabe. Because it does not count some short recitatives as separate movements, it has 47 movements. Alternative movements are part of the Bärenreiter edition.

A gentle introduction to the forms of music in *Messiah*

It will be helpful to make a few comments about the forms of music to be found within the oratorio, without making them too technical. Apologies are offered to readers who feel that this section is too technical and that the inclusion in the heading of the word 'gentle' is misplaced.

Apart from two purely instrumental movements (the 'Overture' of Movement 1 and the 'Pastoral Symphony' of Movement 13), all the movements make use of voices and belong to one of three types: *accompagnatos* (or recitatives), airs and choruses.

---

[7] Mozart, *Der Messias,* K.572. The arrangement was produced in 1789 and published in 1803.

Accompagnatos and recitatives

Movements described as *accompagnato* (such as Movement 2) or recitative (for example, Movement 8) consist of a solo vocal composition in which ordered melody, rhythm and metre are largely disregarded in favour of some imitation of the natural inflections of speech. Movements marked recitative are accompanied by only the *continuo* (which means an independent bass line, usually filled out with chords, played by a keyboard instrument – this would have been the harpsichord or organ in Handel's time). Recitatives marked *accompagnato* are accompanied by additional string instruments. However, in some editions of *Messiah* the term 'recitative' is used for both variations. *Accompagnatos* and recitatives are normally short and often function as a lead-in to an air or chorus.

Airs

Another word for an air is the Italian word *aria*. It denotes a solo vocal piece of melodious character – what we might call a song. One of the airs is in the form of a duet – *'O death, where is thy sting?'* (Movement 50). Another air – Movement 20 – although labelled as a duet, has the two voices singing successive halves of the item, not singing together.

Some airs, such as the first air of the oratorio, *'Every valley shall be exalted'* (Movement 3) adopt the pattern of the binary form, which was commonly used in Baroque music. This means that the air falls into two halves of more or less equal length, although the two halves are not totally identical. In this particular air, the first half starts in the home key of E major and modulates into the closely related key of B major. The two halves are linked by a bridge passage. In the second half, the development of the tune is somewhat different: modulating back into B major but, for the most part, in the home key of E major.

Not all airs in *Messiah* have a binary form, but many do. One variation on the basic pattern is found in *'He shall feed his flock like a shepherd'* (Movement 20), where the two halves are sung by two different soloists.

The airs of Movement 23 (*'He was despised'*) and Movement 48 (*'The trumpet shall sound'*) have a ternary form (otherwise known as *da capo* airs), in other words, their shape is A-B-A.[8]

Choruses

Choruses are a major feature of *Messiah* and provide the opportunity for a large number of singers who would not dare to perform as a soloist, nevertheless to participate in performances. The sheer body of four-part vocal harmony from a group of singers clearly provides a contrast with *accompagnatos*, recitatives and airs sung by a solo voice, thus adding to the musical interest. Often the chorus items give greater emphasis to the Bible verses being sung, which is particularly appropriate when the words express praise or worship. At other times, the choruses work more reflectively, particularly when the Bible verses convey the feelings or response of a crowd of onlookers. A chorus often ends a scene with dramatic effect, and this happens in every scene of Part I.

Two styles of music are used in the choruses of *Messiah.* One is what can be described as 'block chord' sections (the technical term is 'homophony') – in other words, all voices singing the same words in four-part harmony and in the same rhythm as each other, as happens in a Bach chorale or in a church service when the choir sings a hymn.

The other style is described as 'contrapuntal', which means that a similar musical phrase is sung by different voices, with the musical phrase overlapping between the voices in such a way as to fit into the harmonic progression of the music. Most choruses consist of a combination of these two styles.

There are variations on these styles – for example, when one particular voice sings a phrase of its own, while the other three parts sing an accompanying 'block chord' phrase. This feature is known as *cantus firmus*, in other words, a fixed melody around which the other parts are added. Another variation is where two voices work together on a phrase (either in harmony or in unison), while the other two voices work together on a different phrase (again, either in harmony or in unison).

---

[8] The musical direction *da capo* means: Go back to the beginning, start again and continue until you come to the word *Fine* ('End').

One further feature of a number of the choruses is what I like to describe as the 'Handelian hiatus' (although this term is definitely not an official textbook one), namely a dramatic silence, or rest, immediately before the concluding short and stately block chord phrase of the movement. Woe betide the inattentive singer or instrumentalist who fails to follow the conductor and comes in too early!

Part I: From heaven to earth

Part I Scene 1: The Messiah's Coming Means Salvation

1. **'Overture' (or 'Symphony')**
2. **Accompagnato (tenor)**
   Comfort ye, comfort ye my people, saith your God. Speak ye comfortably to Jerusalem, and cry unto her, that her warfare is accomplished, that her iniquity is pardoned. The voice of him that crieth in the wilderness, Prepare ye the way of the Lord, make straight in the desert a highway for our God. (Isaiah 40:1–2a, 3)
3. **Air (tenor)**
   Every valley shall be exalted, and every mountain and hill made low, the crooked straight, and the rough places plain. (Isaiah 40:4)
4. **Chorus**
   And the glory of the Lord shall be revealed, and all flesh shall see it together, for the mouth of the Lord hath spoken it. (Isaiah 40:5)

This first 'scene' of the drama of *Messiah* begins, after the instrumental overture, with settings of most of the first five verses of Isaiah 40, with two questions for the listener. The first is 'Why?' Why does the text begin here of all places? A second question to ask is 'How?' How does this passage of the Old Testament connect us today with Jesus? Both those questions need to be addressed.

Question 1: Why did Charles Jennens choose Isaiah 40:1–5 as his opening text?

Those of us who are familiar with the oratorio are used to hearing the tenor soloist's words of *'comfort'* for God's people. This is more than a casual message of 'Cheer up!' delivered to those who may be feeling out of sorts. These people are at rock bottom, because they are exiles in Babylon, far from their homeland of Judah. Their exile has lasted 70 years. These opening verses of Isaiah 40 are an announcement by God himself of deliverance and rescue for his oppressed people – and it is the coming of the Messiah which will bring about salvation. It is nothing less than the announcement of their release from captivity. This salvation – or *'comfort'* – means that it is none other than *'the Lord', 'our God',* who is bringing his people home. Let's not miss out on the identification of the Messiah, the central figure of the oratorio, with God himself. The Messiah (or Christ) is God's anointed King – his appointment is announced in Psalm 2, as we have seen. He is a divine King who, in his own person, can be called 'God.'

The exile in Babylon was not an accident of history. It was the judgement of God on his people who had persistently disobeyed him and followed false gods. And the punishment of exile fell after repeated warnings from God's prophets, urging the people of God to repent and ask for God's mercy before it was too late. But those warnings fell on spiritually deaf ears. The wayward course of God's people is recorded in the Old Testament narrative. The northern kingdom of Israel fell to the Assyrians in 722 BC. The people were deported, dispersed and lost without trace. 2 Kings 17 in particular spells out the reasons for the judgement on them. The southern kingdom of Judah survived for just over a century more before its people were deported to Babylon, and Jerusalem was destroyed in 587 BC.[1]

What is striking about the Book of Isaiah is that Isaiah ministered in Judah something like 100 years before the Babylonian exile and nearly 200 years before the return from exile. But in chapter 39, he clearly anticipates the exile, and in chapter 40 onwards his focus is on the return from exile.

The content of Isaiah 39 can be told briefly. In 712 BC King Hezekiah received envoys from Babylon and showed them the full extent of his treasures and armaments. The implication is that, on this occasion, Hezekiah (who was one of Judah's more godly kings) fell into the sin of pride and of trusting pagan allies rather than in God. When Isaiah learned what had happened, he declared a word from the Lord: at a future date, Babylon, far from providing help, would be their oppressor and their

---

[1] The reader may find it helpful to refer to the table of selected dates in biblical history (in Appendix 2 at the end) both here and in connection with further comments on events during the Old Testament period.

place of exile. The king's spiritual malaise was symptomatic of the nation as a whole. For this reason, the disaster to come would be a national one.

Isaiah 40 marks a turning point in this book of the Bible. No sooner has the message of judgement been announced (39:5–7), than Isaiah announces a message of comfort (40:1–2). This message of hope for the future beyond the exile continues to be spelt out in the whole of the remaining chapters of the book. Isaiah wants his own generation to know that God has plans and purposes that will come to fruition, and he wants future generations to be assured of God's unchanging commitment to his promises, so that whether they are in Judah or in Babylon, they will learn to trust him. God will fulfil his promises to Abraham that through him all the nations of the earth will be blessed (Gen 12:1–3). He will raise up the offspring of David and establish the throne of his kingdom for ever, as he promised in 2 Samuel 7:12–14.

We are now in a better position to answer the 'Why?' question of a little earlier: Why does the text of *Messiah* begin in these verses from Isaiah 40? It is because we have here a clear statement that God, in his holiness and justice, must punish his people for their sin. They have endured a long period of exile as the just consequence of their rebellion. But these verses look forward to the time when their sentence has been served. God will act again, but this time in mercy. The Messiah's coming means salvation for his people: he himself will bring them home again.

Before we look at how this passage connects us today with Jesus, we look more closely at the message of *'comfort'*. In Movement 2, we hear God, through Isaiah, speaking *'comfort'* to those whom he still calls *'my people'*. The repetition of the command is a mark of intensity and urgency. The Hebrew for 'to comfort' carries the thought of 'to cause to breathe again'. So there is a strong indication of a new beginning: they are beginning a new life. At the same time, there is an unmistakable note of compassion in God's attitude to his people. The word *'comfort'* is reinforced by the word *'comfortably'*, describing the way God's people are to be addressed. ESV uses the word 'tenderly'. The meaning is 'speaking to the heart'. This tone, together with Israel being spoken of in the feminine form, suggests the way a man might woo his intended bride. Here we see the very heart of God, who dearly loves his wayward people. Their *'warfare'* (AV) or 'hard service' (NIV) – their experience of the appointed period of hardship – has come to an end. Their *'iniquity is pardoned'* (AV) or 'paid for' (NIV), so that justice can be seen to have been done.

Handel's oratorio omits the second half of verse 2, which reads: 'that she has received from the Lord's hand double for all her sins.' This omission was commented on in the Introduction. How many who hear performance of *Messiah* notice the absence of this half-verse? We cannot be sure why Jennens decided to make this editorial cut. Possibly it was because he intended the Messiah's sin-bearing role to be dealt with more fully in Part II of the oratorio. But having brought the missing second half of verse 2 into the discussion, it may be helpful to explain that the reference to receiving 'double for all her sins' does not mean that the people of Judah have suffered twice as severely as they should have done, but rather that there has been an exact equivalence. A useful illustration is a rectangular sheet of paper which is folded double, one side matching the other exactly: the punishment has been sufficient.

Question 2: How does this passage connect us today with Jesus?

Many who hear a performance of *Messiah* may not naturally make the link between these opening verses from Isaiah 40 and Jesus. So it is important that we should grasp how insightful Charles Jennens's choice of text is in order to show us how the coming of Jesus the Messiah means salvation for his people today.

A helpful way into getting to grips with this is to ask ourselves: When did the exile end? It is true that, in a partial way, the promised *'comfort'* came to God's people in 539 or 538 BC when, under God's sovereign control, Cyrus (King of Persia) defeated the Babylonians and issued a decree that all people previously deported could return to their homelands (Ezra 1). So that was the end of the Babylonian exile.

But Isaiah 40 and the following chapters talk of something far bigger than just the return of the Jewish exiles to their homeland under Zerubbabel and the subsequent restoration under Ezra and Nehemiah. That 'something bigger' anticipated here is nothing less than the coming of Jesus. When Jesus came into this world and went to the cross as our Saviour, he was bringing to an end a much more serious exile than the one experienced by the people of Judah in the sixth century BC.

The real exile began in Genesis 3, when Adam and Eve were ejected from the Garden of Eden following their rebellious act of disobedience. From that moment on, the whole human race became alienated from God's presence, cut off from him by sin. The disastrous result of sin, in particular the enmity between God and man, could only be dealt with by the promised offspring of the woman, who would crush the serpent's head (Gen 3:15). Jesus is that offspring, the Messiah, and he brought about the end of the real exile. So that is how the promise of Isaiah 40:1–2 connects us today with Jesus.

It is significant that Simeon, in Luke 2:25, is introduced as 'waiting for the consolation of Israel', which must be regarded as a deliberate echo of the *'comfort'* of Isaiah 40:1. Very near the end of Part I of *Messiah*, we hear Jesus' promise of *'rest'* to those who come to him (Matt 11:28): here too is an echo of that *'comfort'* spoken of here. The opening verses of Isaiah 40 find their 'full' fulfilment (if it may be termed in that way) in Jesus.

The next key concept in this section is *'The voice in the wilderness'* (Isa 40:3–4) – or, as the ESV translates it, 'A voice cries: "In the wilderness"'. Both ways of interpreting these words are admissible. The *'voice'* is clearly identified in the New Testament as John the Baptist (Matt 3:3, Mark 1:2–4, Luke 3:3–6), who indeed acts as herald announcing the Christ's imminent coming at the end of the 'exile'. John himself understood his role in this way (John 1:23). The herald's announcement is that the Lord – *'our God'* himself – is coming to his people in person. Indeed, he is called by his personal name, *'the Lord'* (*Yahweh*), which is signified whenever the word 'Lord' is found in the Old Testament text in capital letters. There are echoes here of the Exodus, when God announced to Moses, 'I have come down to deliver them' (Exod 3:8).

No obstacle will be allowed to obstruct *'the way of the Lord'*: depressions are to be filled in, high ground levelled, rough areas smoothed out. This is pictorial language and can be regarded as the Old Testament equivalent of motorway construction. It is speaking about repentance. God's people cannot properly prepare the way of the Lord without radically turning their minds and hearts and wills from sin. It is true that the miracle of a change of heart cannot take place without the miracle of the Spirit's transforming grace and power. Nevertheless, the command to repent is the essential first step in the proclamation of the gospel, just as it was in John's and Jesus' ministry (Mark 1:4 and 1:15). The wonderful truth that such change is possible and will take place at the Messiah's coming is celebrated in the tenor soloist's air in Movement 3.

The final concept in this section is *'The glory of the Lord'* (Isa 40:5). The first chorus of *Messiah,* in Movement 4, announces the goal of the coming of the Christ: *'And the glory of the Lord shall be revealed'.* The apostle John witnessed the fulfilment of this prophecy, telling us, 'And the Word became flesh and dwelt among us, and we have seen his glory, glory as of the only Son from the Father, full of grace and truth' (John 1:14). Here is an individual who is a real human being and has been made 'flesh'. But, at the same time, because he is the eternal Word of God and the Son from the Father, his glory cannot be hidden. His glory is revealed in his works of power – for example, when he 'manifested his glory' at the wedding at Cana (John 2:11). Supremely, however, his glory is revealed in the cross and resurrection (John 12:27–28; Phil 3:21). The coming of the Messiah was a public event. As Paul could say to Festus and Agrippa of the death and rising again of Jesus, 'This has not been done in a corner' (Acts 26:26).

There is still more to be said about the revealing of the glory of the Lord, for *'all flesh shall see it together'.* The coming of the Messiah is an event which benefits not just one nation (Israel) but of people of all nations. *'All flesh'* means nothing less than that. God's original promise to Abraham was that in him 'all the families of the earth' should be blessed (Gen 12:3). From that point on, we can trace through the Old Testament the golden thread of the promise of God's blessing to the world. As those who live in New Testament days, we can rejoice that the gospel has indeed been preached to the nations of the world – a theme to which we shall return later in Handel's oratorio.

How can we be assured that God will keep his promise? The answer is: solely on the grounds that *'the mouth of the Lord has spoken it'.* At the beginning of the Bible, God said, 'Let there be light' and there was light (Gen 1:3). Today, we can look back at so many of God's fulfilled promises, not least in the coming of Christ and the finished work of the cross, but we can have equal assurance about his still-to-be-fulfilled promises, such as the second coming of Christ. 'The Lord is not slow to fulfil his promise' (2 Pet 3:9); 'God has said it, I believe it, that settles it!', as the well-known saying puts it. But we need to bear in mind, as many have pointed out, that the first and last parts of that saying are true on their own. If God has said it, that settles it, whether we believe it or not. The middle part tells us what our response should be: it presents us with a challenge to believe.

What to listen out for in the music in Part I Scene 1

1. 'Overture' (or 'Symphony')

It would be a mistake to dismiss this instrumental piece as of little importance. The minor key of the 'Overture' creates a feeling of mournfulness, which prepares the ground for the message of 'comfort' in the following movements.

2. *Accompagnato: 'Comfort ye'*

Whereas the 'Overture' was set in E minor, this item is set in a major key (E). From the very first chord of the movement, the note of hope is established. The tenor soloist's lingering repetitions of the phrases *'Comfort ye my people'* and *'that her iniquity is pardoned'* intensify the force of God's merciful words to his people. The tone changes to one of urgency in the second part of the movement, with the announcement of *'the voice of him that crieth in the wilderness.'*

3. Air: *'Every valley shall be exalted'*

This air illustrates the way Handel so often hides his skill under a cloak of simplicity.

The tune for the opening words *'Every valley'* is announced in the first bar by the first violins as the top line of the orchestral introduction. It simply consists of a rising figure of four of the first five notes of the home key of E major. (In what is known as the 'tonic sol-fa', it is the *do, re, mi* and *so* of the scale, without the *fa*).[2] When the tenor sings that one-bar phrase a few bars later, he does so unaccompanied. The orchestra then repeat their opening bar, and the tenor responds with a further rising figure starting a third higher *(mi, fa, so)*, followed by an upward leap to the top *do.*

A repeated one-bar rising figure, with the repeat pitched slightly higher, is simple enough, but Handel immediately follows it in the very next bar

[2] 'Tonic sol-fa' will be well known to those familiar with *The Sound of Music* from the famous number, 'Do-Re-Mi', sung by Maria and the children. Music by Richard Rodgers and lyrics by Oscar Hammerstein II.

with the tenor descending the whole scale from top E to the lower E (in other words, the top *do* all the way down to the lower *do*) with the words *'shall be exalted'.*

This simple device both establishes the principal motif in the listener's ear and provides the material from which the rest of the tenor's air is developed. It really is craftsmanship of the highest order under the mask of the most basic of musical patterns.

This air also provides a good example of Handel's skilful use of what might be described as 'musical onomatopoeia', in other words painting the words in the way they are sung. So, for example, the word *'exalted'* is often rendered by extended *coloraturas,* meaning that the melody for that word is in the form of decorated runs. By contrast, the word *'low'* in the phrase *'and every mountain and hill made low'* is given a low note. *'Plain'* is often depicted with a long note, and a complicated figure is used for *'crooked'.* The technique is so basic but extremely effective.

4. Chorus: *'And the glory of the Lord shall be revealed'*

One particular feature to note is the sopranos' *cantus firmus* (the fixed melody around which other parts are added) on the words *'for the mouth of the Lord hath spoken it'* while, beneath them, the other three parts sing *'and all flesh shall see it together'.* This particular instance of *cantus firmus* serves as another example of 'musical onomatopoeia', as it can be seen as an illustration of God's majesty and his words (*'the mouth of the Lord'*) taking control of the music.

Part I Scene 2: The Messiah's Coming Means Judgement

5. *Accompagnato* **(bass)**
   Thus saith the Lord of hosts: Yet once, a little while, and I will shake the heavens, and the earth, the sea, and the dry land; and I will shake all nations, and the desire of all nations shall come. (Haggai 2:6–7a)
   The Lord, whom ye seek, shall suddenly come to his temple, even the messenger of the covenant, whom ye delight in; behold, he shall come, saith the Lord of hosts. (Malachi 3:1b)
6. **Air (contralto)**
   But who may abide the day of his coming, and who shall stand when he appeareth? For he is like a refiner's fire. (Malachi 3:2a)
7. **Chorus**
   And he shall purify the sons of Levi, that they may offer unto the Lord an offering in righteousness. (Malachi 3:3b, 3d)

Salvation and judgement

Jennens clearly intended this second scene to contrast with the opening one. He has already unpacked something of the Messiah's role in bringing salvation, and he now develops the theme of the judgement which will fall on the world and from which the Messiah will deliver his people. Jennens's original heading for the first of these two opening scenes is: (1) 'Isaiah's prophecy of salvation'. In a somewhat wordy turn of phrase, he entitles the second: (2) 'The prophecy of the coming Messiah and the question, despite (1), of what this may portend for the World.'[1] These examples, particularly the one for Scene 2, provide solid evidence as to why Jennens's original titles are no longer used today! His meaning is simply 'The coming of the Messiah means judgement' – we might wish he had said so a little more straightforwardly.

[1] See Appendix 1.

The Old Testament prophecies about the coming of the Messiah tell us that he will bring both salvation and judgement. The Old Testament's anticipation of 'the day of the Lord' similarly include both aspects. Often the two strands are placed alongside each other or intertwined, as if hand in hand. The New Testament, however, tells us that there are two comings of the Christ: his first coming which took place 2,000 years ago, and his second coming which still lies in the future. In addition, the New Testament enables us to see how salvation and judgement each belong properly to the two different comings.

The purpose of his first coming is bringing salvation: 'For God so loved the world, that he gave his only Son, that whoever believes in him should not perish but have eternal life. For God did not send his Son into the world to condemn the world, but in order that the world might be saved through him' (John 3:16–17).

Judgement still belongs to the future, second coming of Christ. We see this, for example, in Jesus' clear statement in Matthew 25:31–32 about his role on his return – and this is only one example of many. Jesus speaks clearly and urgently about the judgement to come more frequently and more graphically than anyone else in Scripture. And it needs to be pointed out that it is in this life that the final outcome (salvation or judgement, heaven or hell) is decided for every individual person:

> Whoever believes in him is not condemned, but whoever does not believe is condemned already, because he has not believed in the name of the only Son of God. And this is the judgement: the light has come into the world, and people loved the darkness rather than the light because their deeds were evil (John 3:18–19).

In view of all this, Jennens was right to include a scene which focuses on the theme of judgement.

Shaking of all the nations

Scene 2 opens with Movement 5, consisting of a bass *accompagnato*. The first part of it uses the words of Haggai 2:6–7a. The prophet Haggai exercised his ministry in the late sixth century BC, at the time of the return of the first wave of Jewish exiles to their homeland following the

Babylonian exile. Their leaders were Zerubbabel (the governor) and Joshua (the high priest). Haggai's prophecies can all be dated on the basis of internal evidence as 520 BC. Haggai 2:6–7 belongs to the third of Haggai's five 'oracles' in the book. In this one, he encourages the leaders and the people to get on with the work of rebuilding the temple. In words which echo God's repeated command to the earlier Joshua, he says, 'Be strong ... Work, for I am with you, declares the Lord of hosts. ... My Spirit remains in your midst' (Hag 2:4–5).

Then come the words used in the first part of Movement 5. *'Yet once, a little while'* means 'Wait, just a little while'. God is saying that it will not be long before he begins to *'shake the heavens, and the earth, the sea, and the dry land'* (v 6). He will *'shake all nations'* (v 7). The tense used indicates that he will cause a series of shakings. The image conjures up pictures of earthquakes, by no means uncommon in Old Testament Israel, and the image points to God's supernatural intervention. A number of prophets speak of God's judgement to come in these terms. Earthquakes are an apt symbol of God's judgement, coming as they do without warning and offering little chance of escape from the destruction they bring.

Jennens obviously understood the words he selected from Haggai 2 to point to the judgement to come, and that is correct. But there is more to this prophecy than the future day of judgement on the ungodly – and it may be that Jennens was unaware of the full meaning of these verses because of the wording of the AV at this point. A more accurate translation of this verse was not available to people in the eighteenth century. Today, we can read a more precise rendering of the original text of Haggai 2:7 in a version such as the ESV. The whole of that verse, not just the first part which Jennens uses, is translated as: 'And I will shake all nations, so that the treasures of all nations shall come in, and I will fill this house with glory, says the Lord of hosts.' God is encouraging his people that he will carry out his 'shaking' with the result that 'the treasures of all nations shall come in' to help with the adorning of the temple.

There is little doubt that, for Jennens and his contemporaries, *'the desire of the nations'* (translated as 'the treasures of all nations' in the ESV) was understood as a title for the Messiah. For many of us today who have grown up on the AV, it is a familiar and cherished title for Jesus. However, as the verb 'shall come in' is plural, a plural subject makes better sense.

For this reason, the ESV's 'the treasures' (or RV's 'desirable things') is to be preferred.

So it will be clear that, while Haggai 2:6–7 is looking ahead to the judgement to come, the verse also has something to say about the more immediate future for God's people who have returned to Judah. The message for them is one of encouragement. It is an assurance that the resources they need for the work of rebuilding the temple will be provided.

It may appear puzzling that these two verses in Haggai 2 seem to be referring both to the distant future when God 'will shake all nations' in judgement and also to the more immediate future when 'the treasures of all nations shall come in' as a help towards the rebuilding of the temple. But prophecy in the Old Testament often works like this, offering us a perspective that combines events that belong to different times of what lies ahead. We have already noticed this in connection with the way the Old Testament often seems to combine the first and second comings of Christ. The only essential difference here is that events that lie only a short time ahead are included in this perspective as well.

One illustration that can be helpful in making sense of all this is the view you might have on a clear day from the top of a mountain in the Lake District or the Alps. As you look ahead, you see some peaks in the near distance, others that lie in the middle distance, and still others on the very far horizon. As you look, the whole perspective may appear to merge together, so that mountain tops that are in reality a great distance from each other appear to be adjacent to each other.

It is not always the case that all three aspects of what is to come will be appear in a particular passage of prophecy, but they do in these verses.[2]

We can apply all this to Haggai 2:6–7 and separate out three separate reference points within the whole panorama of the future:

- The foreground – the imminent future: historically, there was some fulfilment of the prophecy of treasure coming into the

[2] We met the same kind of combination of perspectives in the earlier discussion about the end of the exile in Scene 1: in the short term the end of the exile came through Cyrus's decree, but the "real" end of the exile came about with the coming of Christ and his atoning death on the cross.

temple when the Persian king Darius I gave orders around the year 517 BC to Tattenai, the governor of the province Beyond the River, to provide various kinds of material help in the rebuilding of the temple (Ezra 5:6–17).

- The middle ground – the first coming of Christ: it is the words of Haggai 2:7, 'I will fill this house with glory', that point to Jesus' first coming. 'This house' is the temple, where God would meet with his people. But the temple – and all that it stood for – was fulfilled with the coming of Jesus, because it is in him and through him that we today can meet with God on the basis of his one perfect sacrifice of himself for our sins. In John 2:20–21, Jesus speaks of his body as 'the temple'. The apostle John could say of the Word becoming flesh and dwelling among us (just as God dwelt with his people in the Old Testament tabernacle and temple) that 'we have seen his glory' (John 1:14). At the incarnation, God filled the real 'temple' (his Son, Jesus) with glory. It is significant that a literal 'shaking' accompanied both the death of Jesus, when the curtain of the Jerusalem temple was torn from top to bottom, and also the resurrection of Jesus (Matt 27:51; Matt 28:2).
- The far horizon – the second coming of Christ: Revelation 21:22–24 looks forward to the day when the New Jerusalem will be filled with the presence of God, 'for its temple is the Lord God the Almighty and the Lamb ... and the kings of the earth will bring their glory into it'. Let's notice also the echo of 'the treasures of the nations' that shall come in. This perspective on the glory of heaven, suggested by Haggai 2:6–7, is reinforced by the way those verses are used in Hebrews 12:26–29. God's shakings of the physical universe will usher in 'a kingdom that *cannot be shaken*' (my italics) – the climax to a section that speaks of the glorious worship of the heavenly Jerusalem.

How does the long-term fulfilment of God's promise at the second coming of Christ square with the promise of *'a little while'* in Haggai 2:6? The answer must be that we should beware of impatiently imposing our human timescale on God's perfectly regulated calendar. That was the mistake made by those in the apostle Peter's generation who dismissed the promise of the Lord's return because it had not yet happened. Peter gives us the right perspective:

> But do not overlook this one fact, beloved, that with the Lord one day is as a thousand years, and a thousand years as one day. The Lord is not slow to fulfil his promise as some count slowness, but is patient towards you, not wishing that any should perish, but that all should reach repentance (2 Peter 3:8–9).

In C S Lewis's *The Voyage of the Dawn Treader,* there is an instructive conversation between Lucy and Aslan (who represents Christ): '"Please, Aslan", said Lucy, "what do you call *soon*?" "I call all times soon", said Aslan.'[3]

So while Haggai 2:6–7 point us clearly to the reality of judgement, these verses (rightly understood) also point us to the glory of the Messiah, both in his incarnation and in his future appearing.

The messenger of the covenant

Jennens uses parts of Malachi 3:1–3 for the second half of the bass *accompagnato* (Movement 5), the contralto air (Movement 6) and the chorus (Movement 7). The text is selected from Malachi 2:17–3:5. It will be helpful to set out the whole of this six-verse section and highlight the parts that Jennens incorporates:

> 2:17 You have wearied the Lord with your words. But you say, 'How have we wearied him?' By saying, 'Everyone who does evil is good in the sight of the Lord, and he delights in them.' Or by asking, 'Where is the God of justice?'
>
> 3:1 Behold, I send my messenger, and he will prepare the way before me. And **the Lord whom you seek will suddenly come to his temple; and the messenger of**

[3] C. S. Lewis, *The Voyage of the Dawn Treader* (Harmondsworth: Penguin Books, 1965), 138–39.

> **the covenant in whom you delight, behold, he is coming, says the Lord of hosts.**
>
> 3:2 **But who can endure the day of his coming, and who can stand when he appears? For he is like a refiner's fire** and like fullers' soap.
>
> 3:3 He will sit as a refiner and purifier of silver, **and he will purify the sons of Levi** and refine them like gold and silver, and **they will bring offerings in righteousness to the Lord.**
>
> 3:4 Then the offering of Judah and Jerusalem will be pleasing to the Lord as in the days of old and as in former years.
>
> 3:5 Then I will draw near to you for judgement. I will be a swift witness against the sorcerers, against the adulterers, against those who swear falsely, against those who oppress the hired worker in his wages, the widow and the fatherless, against those who thrust aside the sojourner, and do not fear me, says the Lord of hosts.

We can only speculate why Jennens did not include the whole of this passage, but the most likely explanation is that he simply went straight to the parts of this section that seemed most suitable to him for the purpose of linking the Messiah's coming with judgement.

It is probable that Malachi prophesied to the people of Judah around 60 years after Haggai, which means that there is a chronological sequence in Jennens's choice of Bible texts in the opening part of the oratorio: first Isaiah, then Haggai, and now Malachi. The shocking thing is that a later generation of the people who returned from exile with high hopes of a new start have to be addressed throughout the Book of Malachi in such words of condemnation as we find here.

In this section, Malachi takes the people to task for harbouring cynical attitudes towards God. To 'have wearied the Lord' with their words (2:17) is a serious charge. The two questions they are reported to have been asking suggest that they believe that sin does not matter. Malachi's answer comes over as God's own words. The God on whom they have turned their backs will himself intervene (just as he promised to do in Haggai 2). God will send two messengers, both of whom are mentioned in Malachi 3:1.

The first is the forerunner, 'my messenger'. He is not included in the oratorio's text. We have already identified this individual as John the Baptist in our earlier discussion of Isaiah 40:1–5. He is the herald (or *'the voice'*).

The second is none other *'the Lord, whom ye seek'*, and he *'shall suddenly come to his temple'*. He too is described as a messenger, but he is different from the first one. He is *'the messenger of the covenant'*. This is a fitting title for the Lord God, who himself has entered into a covenant (or solemnly binding agreement) with his people. Jennens is surely right to see this individual (*'the Lord'*) as the Messiah.[4] Almost certainly there is irony in the phrase *'whom ye seek'*, as also in the words *'whom ye delight in'*. They made an outward show of seeking him and claimed to find delight in doing so, but the reality was a different matter. Malachi exposes their true godlessness which they cloaked under a veneer of spirituality.

The Lord's sudden arrival at his temple finds its fulfilment in the incarnation, as does *'the day of his coming'* in verse 2. But the focus of that coming to his temple can be sharpened by reference to Jesus' sudden arrival at the temple following his triumphal entry into Jerusalem, the ensuing confrontations within the temple precincts with the religious and political leaders of the day, and his fierce denunciation of the scribes and Pharisees (Matt 21:12–23:39; Mark 11:15–12:44; Luke 19:45–20:47). Jesus' visit to the temple during that final week of his ministry is followed by his departure from the temple, making his way to the Mount of Olives, where he foretells the destruction of the temple and Jerusalem at the hands of the Romans.[5]

---

[4] The word used is *adōnāy* ('the Lord' in lower case letters in English versions), not *YHWH* ('the LORD').

[5] That departure is a deliberate echo of the glory of the Lord departing from the temple in Ezekiel 10–11 and standing on the mountain on the east side of the city

Two kinds of judgement

There is another major truth about judgement to be found in these verses in Malachi. We are told that there are two aspects to the activity of the Messiah in judgement. First, there is judgement which can lead to restoration. We might describe this as God's fatherly discipline of his people. Mercy is always available to those who heed the warnings. But, secondly, there is also judgement that is final. It belongs properly to the final judgement, which will fall at Christ's second coming.

First, the judgement which can lead to restoration: we find in this section of the book that, first, he will purify some sinners (3:2–4). These people are described as *'the sons of Levi'*, an appropriate term to use for those who work at the temple. Both the *'refiner's fire'* (which Jennens includes) and the 'fullers' soap' (which he does not) indicate the thoroughness and the severity of that purifying work. When sinners are challenged to repent, the process can be painful, as when having a decaying tooth extracted, but the purpose is a beneficial one. What is in view here is not the judgement which falls on impenitent sinners, but an expression of God's loving fatherly discipline of his children. The writer to the Hebrews tells us that God 'disciplines us for our good, that we may share his holiness. For the moment all discipline seems painful rather than pleasant, but later it yields the peaceful fruit of righteousness to those who have been trained by it' (Heb 12:10b–11).

Referring again to C S Lewis's *The Voyage of the Dawn Treader*, those familiar with the story will recall how Eustace, who has been turned into a dragon, experiences what can only be described as a pictorial representation of what is described in Titus 3:5 as 'the washing of regeneration and renewal of the Holy Spirit'. As part of the process, Eustace has to discover that his own efforts to scratch off the dragon's skin are to no avail, and he has to endure the painful process of Aslan stripping him of the deepest layers. In the story, Eustace tells Edmund what happened:

> The very first tear he made was so deep that I thought
> it had gone right into my heart. And when he began

(in other words, the Mount of Olives) as a prelude to the forthcoming destruction of the temple and Jerusalem at the hands of the Babylonians. There should be no mistaking the intensity of the note of judgement that is conveyed by Malachi 3:1.

> pulling the skin off, it hurt worse than anything I've felt. The only thing that made me able to bear it was just the pleasure of feeling the stuff peel off.[6]

Coming back to the passage of Malachi, we discover the second activity of the Messiah at his coming and the second type of judgement – the judgement which is final. In words which Jennens omits from his text, the Messiah will judge other sinners (3:5). Little is required by way of extra comment. This is judgement with a chilling finality, which is pronounced even here and now on those who persist in hardening their hearts and refusing to repent, even though the sentence will not be exacted until Christ's second coming.

Belief today in judgement is not popular. Perhaps it never has been. John Robinson wrote a number of years ago:

> We live, in this 20th century, in a world without judgement, a world where at the last frontier post you simply go out – and nothing happens. It is like coming to the customs and finding there are none after all. And the suspicion that this is in fact the case spreads fast: for it is what we should all like to believe.[7]

But we cannot read the words of Jesus (or of the New Testament as a whole) without recognising that judgement will be a terrible reality for those who are unprepared, in other words for those who will not repent. The Bible gives absolutely no encouragement to those who would love to believe in any kind of universal salvation.

---

[6] Lewis, *Voyage of the Dawn Treader*, 96.

[7] J. A. T. Robinson, *On Being the Church in the World* (London: SCM Press, 1960), 137.

What to listen out for in the music in Part I Scene 2

5. *Accompagnato: 'Thus saith the Lord of hosts'*

The movement opens in a minor key, which helps create a mood of foreboding. Handel's choice of the bass to sing this *accompagnato* enhances that atmosphere.

Several times, the word *'shake'* in the phrase *'and I will shake'* is rendered in *coloraturas* (the decoration of a vocal melody in the shape of runs and similar embellishments) – another example of 'musical onomatopoeia.' The audience cannot fail to feel something of the impact of God's shaking of the nations. Handel's music gives the strings repeated loud semiquaver chords, which add to a powerfully menacing effect. Towards the end of the movement the music suddenly and dramatically calms to an unaccompanied line on the words *'The Lord, whom ye seek, shall suddenly come to the temple.'*

6. Air: *'But who may abide the day of his coming?'*

It is worth listening out for the varying speeds and tones in this air. It begins with a pensive question, *'But who may abide the day of his coming?'* in a lilting 3/8 rhythm and continues in a sharp change of time and tempo (*prestissimo,* very fast) with the statement *'for he is like a refiner's fire.*[8] In the middle section, forceful downward runs, leaps and trills of the voice are accompanied by fiery figurations in the strings.

Like a *da capo,* the pensive question is repeated, but in a shorter version, giving way once more to a *prestissimo* section. The statement returns a final time after a rest, in an affirming *adagio* (a slow section), before a *prestissimo* postlude rounds off this dramatic scene.

7. Chorus: *'And he shall purify the sons of Levi'*

The significant feature to notice in the chorus of Movement 7 is the development of the main idea as a fugue with *coloraturas* on *'purify',* which may be meant to represent purifying fire. 'Fugue' means the sustained use of counterpoint – each of the four voices singing essentially the same phrase, which is then more or less exactly copied by other parts in succession, while the earlier voices are still singing.

---

[8] 3/8 means that each bar consists of three quavers. So the rhythm is 1-2-3, 1-2-3, etc., with the emphasis each time on the '1.'

Part I Scene 3: The Messiah's Birth is Foretold

8. **Recitative (contralto)**
   Behold, a virgin shall conceive, and bear a son, and shall call his name Emmanuel, God with us. (Isaiah 7:14b; Matthew 1:23)
9. **Air (contralto) and Chorus**
   O thou that tellest good tidings to Zion, get thee up into the high mountain; O thou that tellest good tidings to Jerusalem, lift up thy voice with strength; lift it up, be not afraid; say unto the cities of Judah, Behold your God! (Isaiah 40:9)
   O thou that tellest good tidings to Zion, arise, shine for thy light is come, and the glory of the Lord is risen upon thee. (Isaiah 40:9a, 60:1)
10. ***Accompagnato*** **(bass)**
    For, behold, darkness shall cover the earth, and gross darkness the people; but the Lord shall arise upon thee, and his glory shall be seen upon thee. And the Gentiles shall come to thy light, and kings to the brightness of thy rising. (Isaiah 60:2–3)
11. **Air (bass)**
    The people that walked in darkness have seen a great light: and they that dwell in the land of the shadow of death, upon them hath the light shined. (Isaiah 9:2)
12. **Chorus**
    For unto us a child is born, unto us a son is given; and the government shall be upon his shoulder; and his name shall be called Wonderful, Counsellor, The mighty God, The everlasting Father, The Prince of Peace. (Isaiah 9:6)

A virgin shall conceive

Movement 8 opens this scene with a contralto singing the words of the promise of a virgin conception and birth. The promise of Isaiah 7:14 comes in the context of a meeting between the prophet Isaiah and Ahaz, king of Judah, which can be dated about 735 BC, at a time when Assyria – already renowned for its cruelty and oppression – was the rising superpower of the Middle East. Ahaz found himself torn between either joining an alliance against Assyria or submitting to Assyria. Both courses of action were fraught with danger. But when Isaiah met Ahaz, he declared that Ahaz's real choice lay between trusting mere human means of support and trusting God. It was not a political decision, but a spiritual one. If he chose either of the merely 'human' strategies, he would be acting out of fear and desperation. How much better to look to God for his wisdom and help. Basically, the choice was between fear and faith – a foolish fear of man, or a well-founded faith in God. As God said through Isaiah a few chapters earlier, 'Stop regarding man in whose nostril is breath, for of what account is he?' (Isa 2:22). Now God told Isaiah to say to Ahaz, 'Be careful, be quiet, do not fear, and do not let your heart be faint' (Isa 7:4), and 'If you are not firm in faith, you will not be firm at all' (Isa 7:9).

It is at this point in the encounter that Isaiah announced an amazing offer to Ahaz from God: Ahaz was to ask God for a sign, 'let it be deep as Sheol or high as heaven' (v 11). God was acting graciously to Ahaz. If Ahaz was inclined to reject the word of God calling him to trust, God was willing to offer him any sign as a guarantee of his word. But Ahaz refused the gracious offer under the pious pretext of not wanting to put the Lord to the test. The truth, however, was that he was hardening his heart against God.

God's response through Isaiah was that he would give Ahaz a sign anyway: '*Behold, a virgin shall conceive and bear a son, and shall call his name Immanuel*' (v 14b, AV). Matthew 1:22–23 makes it crystal clear that the prophecy is fulfilled in the birth of Jesus, and Matthew's quotation of Isaiah 7:14 gives the explanatory comment about the meaning of the name *'Immanuel'* – *'God with us'*.[1] This was not a prophecy for Ahaz's lifetime, such that he could recognise and understand. No amount of signs could have made any impression on such a hardened heart as Ahaz's. It is as if Isaiah, with his keen prophetic eye, looks across the centuries to the birth of '*Immanuel*'. In so doing, he reminds us of the true perspective of the Old Testament, namely the preparation for the

[1] The AV adopts the spelling 'Immanuel' in Isaiah 7:14 but 'Emmanuel' in Matthew 1:23.

fulfilment of God's promise to provide the ideal king to sit on David's throne. That king would be none other than God himself: the Messiah.

Commentators have expended a large quantity of ink in their discussions as to whether the word translated as *'virgin'* really carries this meaning or, instead, could be translated as 'young woman'. However, we can be assured that Isaiah chose from the words available to him the one which came closest to expressing 'virgin birth' (or 'virgin conception').

The watchman will announce good news

For the contralto air (Movement 9) that follows, Jennens turns first to Isaiah 40:9.[2] He has already quarried the first five verses of this great chapter in Scene 1. In verse 9, Isaiah paints a picture for us. In the excitement attending the coming of the Messiah, a watchman is dispatched to a hilltop to report what he can see. In the context of the chapter, we have to imagine that he can see a great procession coming back from Babylon, as the Lord himself comes across the desert, leading his people home from exile to Jerusalem. He is to shout the news at the top of his voice: 'Here is your God!' (or *'Behold your God!'*). This is indeed *'good tidings'* or 'good news'.

The light will shine in the darkness

The same air (Movement 9) moves straight into another verse from Isaiah, 60:1 – slightly disguised by introducing it with the phrase *'O thou that tellest good tidings to Zion'*, repeated from the text immediately preceding it (Isa 40:9). The context of Isaiah 60 is the future glory of God's people, and Jennens is surely right to link this prospect with the Messiah's coming. Jennens introduces here the important Biblical theme of darkness and light. The *'light'* of *'the glory of the Lord'* will be something for his people to experience themselves, for it is *'thy light'* (Zion being addressed). *'Thy light'* is probably best understood as a parallelism of *'the glory of the Lord'*. But, for those of us today who hold a New Testament in our hands, the phrase anticipates Jesus' own description of himself as 'the light of the world' who brings light and life to his people. He says, 'I am the light of the world. Whoever follows me

---

[2] Jennens follows the marginal alternatives *'O thou that tellest good tidings to Zion/to Jerusalem'* instead of the AV's preferred *'O Zion'* and *'O Jerusalem.'*

will not walk in darkness, but will have the light of life' (John 8:12). *'The glory of the Lord'* is an echo of the same phrase which we heard in Scene 1 from Isaiah 40:5.

More on the light that will shine in the darkness

Movement 10 is a bass *accompagnato* and continues the text of Isaiah 60 with verses 2 and 3. The darkness–light theme is carried over into these two verses. Although the whole world of mankind will be enveloped in darkness (v 2a), the promise of God's light dawning on his people is given (v 2b, 3). That will lead first to his glory being seen on them, and then to people of all nations (or *'Gentiles'*).

Still more on the light that will shine in the darkness

Jennens clearly wished to continue the darkness–light contrast still further. So, having made use of Isaiah 60:1–3 in the previous two movements, he now turns for the bass air in Movement 11 to Isaiah 9:2. Here again we find an anticipation that the coming of the Messiah will transform darkness into light. One striking feature of this Bible verse (and many others in this section) is that the promises of the hope to come are so certain that they can be written in the past tense: *'The people who walked in darkness have seen a great light'*.[3]

The beginning of chapter 9 marks a sudden change:

> But there will be no gloom for her who was in anguish. In the former time he brought into contempt the land of Zebulun and the land of Naphtali, but in the latter time he has made glorious the way of the sea, the land beyond the Jordan, Galilee of the nations' (Isa 9:1).

In 9:2, Isaiah takes us into the well-known words that Jennens uses for the bass air of Movement 11: *'The people that walked in darkness have seen a great light: and they that dwell in the land of the shadow of death,*

---

[3] The context of Isaiah 9 is darkness and gloom. If Jennens had not already given us the theme of darkness in his use of Isaiah 60:2, he might have chosen the last verse of the previous chapter: 'And they will look to the earth, but behold, distress and darkness, the gloom of anguish. And they will be thrust into thick darkness' (Isa 8:22).

upon them hath the light shined.' The northern lands of Zebulun and Naphtali (v 1) covered the area west and south-west of the Sea of Galilee. They were the first part of the Promised Land to fall to Assyria in 733 BC.[4] But verse 1 promises that the dawn will break in the very region that was the first to experience God's judgement.

Gospel-writer Matthew often draws our attention to the ways that Jesus fulfils Old Testament prophecy. It is no surprise, therefore, that he tells us that it was in these northern parts (with their mixed population of Jews and Gentiles) that Jesus first proclaimed the gospel (Matt 4:12–17). Matthew quotes Isaiah 9:1–2 and tells us that Jesus was deliberately fulfilling this prophecy. Most Bible versions in English use the phrase 'Galilee of the Gentiles' in Matthew 4:15 to translate Isaiah's 'Galilee of the nations'. Both translations give us a clear hint of the worldwide spread of the gospel, which – at this time – still lay in the future. The light of the gospel will shine on the Gentiles and on 'all nations'.

Before moving on to the next movement in *Messiah,* it is important to comment on the frequency and importance of the darkness–light contrast in the Bible as a whole. It will not be possible to do justice to it in this book, and readers will need to consult their concordances to pursue that particular field of study. Suffice it to say that walking in darkness, as God's people had done, meant living their lives not only in ignorance but also under God's judgement. But now, as a result of God's gracious action, his people are brought out of darkness into light. That continues to be the offer of the gospel to people in every generation:

> And this is the judgement: the light has come into the world, and people loved the darkness rather than the light because their works were evil. For everyone who does wicked things hates the light and does not come to the light, lest his works should be exposed. But whoever does what is true comes to the light, so that it may be clearly seen that his works have been carried out in God' (John 3:19–21).

[4] This was eleven years before the fall of the capital, Samaria, in 722 BC.

A child is born, a son is given

Although Jennens omits verses 3–5 of Isaiah 9, he gives us verse 6 in Movement 12 (the much-loved chorus, *'For unto us a child is born'*). Handel has produced a stirring item in this particular chorus, which deserves its popularity at Christmas. Personally, I like to hear it at other times of the year too! It provides a truly fitting conclusion to this scene, rounding off the introductory material of the oratorio.

Only two chapters on from the prophecy of the virgin's son (7:14), whose name will be called 'Immanuel', Isaiah 9:6 identifies this son as the promised messianic King and spells out further names by which he may be known (quite apart from the name of 'Jesus', which itself means 'The Lord will save'). The preceding three verses (9:3–5), which Jennens has not given us, explain that the 'light' which God's people will enjoy in place of the previous 'darkness' will mean a release from oppression and the end of all warfare.

Such a transformation begs a question: who will bring about such a salvation? The answer is that all this will happen by the king's birth (v 6): *'For unto us a child is born, unto us a son is given'*. The fact that he is a *'child'* tells us that he is of human descent, while *'son'* emphasises a royal line. Verse 4 has told us that his people's 'shoulders' that have borne the burden of oppression are delivered by his 'shoulder', as he accepts the burden of rule.

The names that this son is given reflect his character (as is so often the case with names in the Bible). Four names are spelt out:

- *'Wonderful, Counsellor'*: the AV puts a comma between these two words, but modern English translations rightly take these two words together. This king has the essential qualification for ruling. *'Wonderful'* has the idea of 'supernatural'; his wisdom, qualifying him to be a *'Counsellor'*, is far above the limited human kind, and there is a world of difference here from the foolish King Ahaz, whom we met in Isaiah 7 and whose decisions ruined his people.
- *'The mighty God'*: this child is the Lord himself, so while he is human he is also divine. He has all power.

- *'The everlasting Father'*: This king will never fade away – his rule is for ever. *'Father'* does not indicate a confusion of the persons of the Trinity, because the individual in view here is none other than the Son, who is God's king (see Psalm 2:6–7, referred to in the Introduction). But the term speaks of the concern, care and discipline which we associate with fathers at their best.

- *'The Prince of Peace'*: *'peace'* means wholeness and completeness, and not only the ceasing of hostility. An end to hostility is, of course, wonderful (with the result that the believer can know peace with God in place of his wrath), but the addition of wholeness and completeness gives a richness to our understanding of this king's rule.

We might have wished that Jennens and Handel had given us verse 7 of Isaiah 9 as well, even though we should be grateful for what we have in this chorus as it stands. However, we can read verse 7 for ourselves and discover four extra truths concerning this human–divine Messiah–King, whom we are privileged to know as Jesus:

- there will be 'no end' to his rule – it will last for ever (expanding on the *'everlasting'* of v 6)
- he will sit on David's throne and is therefore the fulfilment of the promise of 2 Samuel 7:12–14
- he will rule with 'justice' and 'righteousness'
- the guarantee of this amazing promise is the 'zeal' of the Lord God himself, in other words his own personal commitment

What can our response be to such a promise, or indeed to such a king? It must surely be to bow to him, and trust him, and obey him!

What to listen out for in the music in Part I Scene 3

9. Air and chorus: *'O thou that tellest good tidings to Zion'*

One particular feature of this movement is the chorus taking over from the solo contralto about halfway through. This no doubt portrays the spreading of the *'good tidings'* to many people.

When the chorus takes over, the sopranos sing essentially the same melody as the solo contralto at the beginning of the movement, but with a significant difference: the first two notes for the solo contralto are a descending fifth (from A down to D), but the first two notes for the sopranos in the chorus are an ascending fourth (from A up to D).[5] This difference makes sense from a technical point of view, given the natural ranges of each voice. One musicologist, Rudolf Steglich, suggests that that this musical interval (which recurs quite often in the oratorio) is a unifying motif within the work.[6] Further obvious occurrences will be noted in due course. Some musicologists are dismissive of Steglich's suggestion, so listeners will have to make up their own minds about it. Personally, I believe it is worth being aware of it, without letting it assume too great an importance.

This is the first time in the oratorio that we find music in 6/8 time, which always gives a swinging effect.[7]

Coloraturas (decorated runs) accent the words *'mountain'* and *'glory'*, and the words *'God'* and *'Lord'* are set in long notes. The purpose with each is to give emphasis.

---

[5] For readers who might be puzzled by this discussion of an 'ascending fourth', it may be helpful to refer to the beginning of the Christmas carol, 'Hark! The Herald Angels Sing'. The upward leap of the very first two notes of the carol (from 'Hark!' to 'the') is an example of an 'ascending fourth.'

[6] Referred to in R. Luckett, *Handel's Messiah: A Celebration* (London, Victor Gollancz, 1992).

[7] 6/8 means that each bar consists of two beats, each made up of three quavers. So the rhythm is 1-2-3, 4-5-6, 1-2-3, 4-5-6, etc., with the main emphasis each time on the '1' and a lesser emphasis on the '4.'

10. *Accompagnato: 'For, behold, darkness shall cover the earth'*

The music of this movement contrasts markedly with the previous one. The mood is distinctly sombre, and this effect is enhanced by a bass soloist (as in Movement 5). It contains a contrast between its first and second halves, in order to express musically the darkness–light theme of the text.

First, there is the representation of darkness from a brooding orchestral introduction and accompaniment to the bass's opening words, *'For behold, darkness shall cover the earth, and gross darkness the people'*. An air of mystery is evoked by the strings playing repeated motifs in major and minor seconds.

Secondly, the theme of light appears as the text reaches the words *'but the Lord shall arise'* and the mood changes from a minor feel to being decidedly more major. From here on, there is a firmer orchestral accompaniment to the somewhat more florid bass line announcing the good news of Isaiah 60:2b–3. The voice sings the words as a *melisma* (one syllable flowering out into a passage of several notes) of two bars, followed by *coloraturas* on *'glory'* and an upward octave leap to proclaim, *'and kings to the brightness of thy rising'*.

11. Air: *'The people that walked in darkness have seen a great light'*

The darkness, of which the bass soloist sings, is illustrated in this movement by the bass and cellos in unison, proceeding in uneven steps. On *"have seen a great light"* the melody begins to leap and finally reaches the word *"light"* on a long high note which the voice holds, while the cellos continue their movement. The final occurrence of *"darkness"* is a broken downward melisma on the first syllable of the word ("melisma" is explained above), and a few bars later there is an extended vocal decoration on *"light."* In the second half of the verse, the gloom of the beginning is intensified by another melisma, this time on the first syllable of the phrase *"shadow of death."* But the phrase *"upon them hath the light shined"* immediately restores a mood of relief. There are similarities between the opening and closing parts of the music, reflecting the parallel thoughts of the two halves of the Bible-verse.

12. Chorus: *'For unto us a child is born'*

With the marking *piano* (in other words, quiet), the sopranos are the first to enter with the theme of a fugue.[8] It is a delicate theme with many rests. After the tenors make their entry, the sopranos' countersubject (in other words, a second theme, contrasting with the opening theme) is a shimmering *coloratura* for more than three bars, and it is echoed by the basses.

The words *'and the government shall be upon his shoulders'* appear in stately dotted rhythm. This culminates in the four names of the *'son'* in block chord from all four voices, with the earlier shimmering *coloratura* in the strings. The full text is repeated a second and third time, with variations from the first statement. The chorus ends triumphantly with a fourth round, this time with the theme in the bass and the countersubject in soprano and contralto in parallel thirds.

[8] See Movement 7 for an explanation of this term.

Part I Scene 4: The Messiah's Birth is Announced to the Shepherds

13. **'Pastoral Symphony'**
14. **a) Recitative (soprano)**
    There were shepherds abiding in the field, keeping watch over their flock by night. (Luke 2:8)
    b) *Accompagnato* (soprano)
    And lo, the angel of the Lord came upon them and the glory of the Lord shone round about them; and they were sore afraid. (Luke 2:9)
15. **Recitative (soprano)**
    And the angel said unto them, Fear not: for, behold, I bring you good tidings of great joy, which shall be to all people. For unto you is born this day in the city of David a Saviour, which is Christ the Lord. (Luke 2:10–11)
16. ***Accompagnato* (soprano)**
    And suddenly there was with the angel a multitude of the heavenly host praising God, and saying, (Luke 2:13)
17. **Chorus**
    Glory to God in the highest, and peace on earth, good will toward men. (Luke 2:14)

'Pastoral Symphony'

In dramatic terms, the 'Pastoral Symphony' provides a pause between the opening scenes of prophetic preparation and the decisive events of God entering into the world he had made in the person of his own Son – 'fullness of God in helpless babe', in the words of Stuart Townend's hymn 'In Christ Alone'. C S Lewis, in his book *Miracles*, marvellously describes the incarnation as *The Grand Miracle.*[1] In *The Last Battle*, Lewis puts a thought-provoking sentence on the lips of Lucy when she says, 'In our

[1] C. S. Lewis, *Miracles* (Glasgow: Collins/Fount, 1977), 112.

world ... a Stable once had something inside it that was bigger than our whole world.'[2]

The 'Pastoral Symphony' is sometimes said to depict the calm of the first Christmas Eve. If Handel had in mind an idyllic world at peace, rather like a Dickensian Christmas card scene, this would be a misrepresentation of the true state of the world at any time since the Fall. However, it is more helpful to imagine the world immediately before Jesus' birth, preoccupied with its regular activities, totally unaware of the momentous event about to take place. It is the same situation that Jesus describes, when he says, "For as in the days before the flood they were eating and drinking, marrying and giving in marriage, until the day when Noah entered the ark, and they were unaware until the flood came and swept them all away, so will be the coming of the Son of Man" (Mt.24.38-39). People in Noah's day were occupied with the ordinary activities of human life, which were good in themselves, but they were unmindful of the *judgement* about to engulf them. People who will be alive in the period immediately before Jesus' Second Coming will similarly have no thought for the *judgement* about to come. A future Day of Judgement is a reality for every generation, whether or not they are prepared for it. But the tragedy to be noted here is that, by and large, people on earth 2000 years ago had no thought for Jesus' imminent First Coming, which would announce an offer of *mercy*. After all, Jesus speaks of how 'in those days before the flood they were eating and drinking, marrying and giving in marriage', (Matt 24:38). He continues: ' and they were unaware until the flood came and swept them all away, so will be the coming of the Son of Man' (Matt 24:39). If people could be occupied with the ordinary activities of human life, good in themselves, when they were under judgement at the flood and can do so again when judgement will come at Jesus' second coming, the same was certainly true 2,000 years ago at Jesus' merciful first coming.

The well-known Christmas carol 'It Came Upon the Midnight Clear' by Edward Hamilton Sears probably strikes the right balance, when it says:

[2] C. S. Lewis, *The Last Battle* (Harmondsworth: Penguin Books, 1964), 128.

> The world in solemn stillness lay
> to hear the angels sing.[3]

Perhaps, then, we should hear a representation of that 'solemn stillness' in the 'Pastoral Symphony'. But that same carol also goes on to remind us of the real human condition both then and now:

> With sorrow brought by sin and strife
> the world has suffered long,
> and, since the angels' song, have passed
> two thousand years of wrong.

The message of the angels, soon to be announced in *Messiah,* only makes sense against the background of 'man at war with man', to quote again from that carol, as well as mankind at war with God.

The angel of the Lord's announcement to the shepherds

This scene provides us with the only extended 'action' from the Gospels in the whole oratorio, and it focuses on the angel's announcement of Christ's birth to the shepherds. In four consecutive recitative sections (Movements 14–16), the soprano narrates Luke 2:8–11, 13. Luke 2:12 is omitted – more about that in the next section of this chapter.

Luke's account of the birth of Jesus is full of surprises, many of which may well pass us by because of our familiarity with the event. One particular surprise is that God should have chosen shepherds to be the first people to receive the official birth announcement. They are privileged to hear it from none other than the angel of the Lord, attended by heaven's angelic army. ('Army' is the proper meaning of the word *'host'* and should cause us to reflect whether we tend to domesticate these awesome messengers of God). On top of this, the shepherds are summoned to be the first witnesses of the baby Messiah (Luke 2:12).

Why is it a surprise? Because not only were shepherds at the bottom of the social hierarchy, they were generally thought of as being unreliable and inclined to thieving. The fact that their line of work prevented them from observing the ceremonial law did nothing to enhance their

[3] Edward Hamilton Sears, 'It Came Upon the Midnight Clear' in *Christian Register* (Boston, 1849) Vol.28, #52, 206.

reputation. Despite this, we have no reason to believe that the shepherds of Luke 2 were anything other than godly men. In Scene 1, the amazing truth was noted that the gospel of Jesus Christ is for people of all nations, but equally amazing is the truth that the gospel is for people of all backgrounds.

Almost every word in the angel's message in Luke 2:10–11 is significant:

- *'Fear not'*: The natural human reaction to the terrifying experience of having the angel of the Lord appearing to you *is* 'to fear'. But they are told to do the exact opposite!
- *'for, behold, I bring you good tidings'*: this is what the word 'gospel' means – good news. In fact, the best news that could ever be passed on.
- *'of great joy'*: here is a message to rejoice the heart.
- *'which shall be to all people'*: in general terms, it is for Jews and Gentiles – for the whole world.
- *'For unto you'*: in specific terms, it is for this group of despised shepherds.
- *'is born'*: the wonder of the Word becoming flesh.
- *'this day'*: after all the centuries of preparation throughout the whole Old Testament period, God is stepping into this world at this particular point of time.
- *'in the city of David'*: the reminder that Jesus is great David's greater Son, the one who fulfils the promise of 2 Samuel 7:12–13.
- *'a Saviour'*: he is the rescuer, announced in Isaiah 40 (as Scene 1 has told us); and the name Jesus means 'the Lord saves' (Matt 1:21).
- *'which is Christ the Lord'*: he is none other than the Messiah, the King.

Few pairs of verses in the whole Bible have so much high-octane theological and evangelistic content packed into them.

Messiah's missing manger

Here is another of Jennens's surprising omissions from the Bible text in the oratorio. Luke 2:12 is missing. This is the verse which provides us with the continuation of the angel's message: 'And this will be a sign for you: you will find a baby wrapped in swaddling cloths and lying in a manger.' It is difficult to understand the reason for this particular gap in the oratorio. Whatever the reason, it is a pity, as an opportunity has been missed to point to the humiliation that Jesus willingly took upon himself, as indicated by that word 'manger'. We cannot rewrite the oratorio, but the following paragraphs will be an attempt to fill the gap.

A recent prayer letter from workers with Wycliffe Bible Translators contained a Christmas story from Nigeria. It concerned the translation into the native language of Luke 2:7, which is the first verse in the passage to refer to the manger. The native translators wanted to choose a particular word in the tribal language, but the translators' consultant discovered that this was the word for an ordinary cradle. When he showed them what the Translators' Handbook had to say on the subject of 'manger', they objected that the word for an ordinary cradle was the one traditionally used by this tribe when they spoke of the events of the first Christmas. The prayer letter continued:

> The consultant explained that it wasn't just a matter of tradition. God expects us to find words that express the original meaning as accurately as possible. Furthermore, this word 'manger' tells us something profound about God. When he came to live among us and bring salvation to us, he came in the lowliest way possible. He did not come and sleep in a nice cradle like every mother wants for her newborn. So the translators needed to find their best word for an animal feeding trough.

This led to the local translators deciding to use the word for an old worn-out basket that is not usable for anything except feeding animals. The next weekend, they read the story of Jesus' birth to various church groups in the local villages, testing out this word to see how people reacted to it. People were visibly moved, as they recognised in a new way that Jesus was willing to do whatever it took to reach them. He did not only wash the disciples' feet and die on the cross. His humility started right from birth.

We might add that we, as readers of Luke 2 today, and as listeners to Handel's *Messiah,* need to make sure that we do not lose a sense of wonder at the amazing contrast between the majesty that rightfully belongs to the Lord Jesus Christ and the humility to which he stooped at his birth.

Glory to God

A chorus (Movement 17) rounds off this scene, singing the hymn of praise of *'the heavenly host'* which is recorded in Luke 2:14. What other response can there be to the birth of the Messiah? The ESV version of this verse is, 'Glory to God in the highest, and on earth peace among those with whom he is pleased' – a verse consisting of three phrases.

The first phrase of the angels' song rightly gives glory to God: 'Glory to God in the highest.'

The second phrase concerns the peace that God offers to the human race: 'and on earth peace'. This peace signifies an end of hostility between God in heaven and mankind on earth, and also it signifies everything associated with the Hebrew word for 'peace' (*shalom*): wholeness and healing. This peace would be achieved by Jesus' death. As the apostle Paul puts it, 'making peace by the blood of his cross' (Col 1:20).

As regards the third phrase, ESV's 'among those with whom he is pleased' is a better translation than the AV's *'good will toward men'*. Peace on earth becomes a reality among those who are redeemed in Christ and on whom his favour rests. It is also a better translation than the popular phrase 'among men of good will', which appears in the Douay–Rheims Bible. Men and women are the recipients of God's good pleasure – it is certainly not the case that the good will comes from mankind.

What to listen out for in the music in Part I Scene 4

13. 'Pastoral Symphony'

The 'Pastoral Symphony', which opens this scene, is the only movement other than the 'Overture' to be scored for instruments only. It is sometimes known as '*Pifa*', which takes its name from the shepherd bagpipers, or *pifferari*, who played their pipes in the streets of Rome at Christmas time. There is a suggestion of the 'drone' effect of bagpipes in the long sustained notes played by the bass instruments of the orchestra. The music is in C major and the movement's swinging 12/8 time makes it gently rise and fall like a cradle song.[4]

14a) Recitative: *'There were shepherds abiding in the field'*

14b) *Accompagnato: 'And lo, the angel of the Lord came upon them'*

15. Recitative: *'And the angel said unto them, Fear not'*

16. *Accompagnato: 'And suddenly there was with the angel'*

The repeated groups of semiquavers from the strings throughout the second part of Movement 14 and in Movement 16 are intended as a representation of the wings of the angel of the Lord as he appears to the frightened shepherds, and of the multitude of angels who join him. However, the Bible is consistently silent on the question whether angels have wings! This is one of the many myths that have developed around the Christmas event, and the only possible reasons for imagining angels with wings would appear to be the cherubim of Exodus 25 (and elsewhere), the seraphim of Isaiah 6 and the living creatures of Ezekiel 1. Are angels to be identified with one or other of these orders of heavenly beings? We do not know. But rather than let this consideration become a major issue, a wiser course is to enjoy the music with its theatrical imaginativeness and, more importantly, to wonder at the stunning message that the angel of the Lord brings.

The soprano soloist is the dominant voice in this scene. As Handel has delayed her first contribution in the oratorio until this point, her entry is all the more striking.

---

[4] 12/8 time means four beats in a bar, each beat consisting of three quavers.

In Movement 15 we find significant use of the upward fourth (found also in Movement 9) in the phrases: *'for behold'*, *'good tidings'*, and *'for unto you'*. Each time, it is followed by a short rest. Both the recurring upward leap and the following rest bring about an emphasis of the phrase each time.

Just before the end of this short recitative, there is a similar upward leap on the phrase *'which is Christ'*. These words are, of course, the most important part of the angel's message – announcing that the newborn baby is none other than the Messiah, and this phrase is particularly emphasised by being an upward leap of one semitone more than a fourth (what is technically known as an augmented fourth).

In Movement 16, the soprano continues to tell of the arrival of *'a multitude of the heavenly host'*. The voice sings further upward fourths on *'And suddenly'* and *'praising God'* – each time followed by a rest – while the music is supported by an even more vibrant accompaniment of the violins.

17. Chorus: *'Glory to God in the highest'*

The phrase *'Glory to God in the highest'* is sung by the sopranos, contraltos and tenors (without the basses) thus creating a lighter effect. This phrase is answered by *'and peace on earth'*, sung by the tenors and basses in unison, with the basses descending an octave from *'and peace'* to *'on earth'*. In this way Handel marks a musical contrast between the heights where God is surrounded by glory and the depths of earth to which peace is given. The opening phrase is repeated, but not in an identical way.

In great contrast, *'good will towards men'* is sung in a fast sequence of entries in imitation, with the word *'good will'* on another upward fourth (that significant unifying motif within this oratorio).

The whole sequence (from *'Glory to God'* to *'towards men'*) is repeated, but this time all four voices sing *'glory'* and *'peace'* – the *'glory'* phrase in a high register, and the *'peace'* phrase low, again with the bass dropping an octave.

After the song, the disappearance of the angels is indicated dramatically by three features in the remaining eight bars of the movement: the first is the *diminuendo* in the instrumentation; the second is the thinning out of the instrumentation with more and more rests; the third is the higher pitch of the violins in the last two bars – suggestive of the angels' return to the heights of heaven.

Trumpets are used in this chorus for the first time in the oratorio. They provide an appropriate accompaniment to an angelic outburst of praise. Handel's use of trumpets in this work is remarkably restrained. After their introduction in this chorus, they are heard only in the 'Hallelujah' Chorus (Part II, Movement 44), in the air 'The trumpet shall sound' (Part III, Movement 48) and the final chorus 'Worthy is the Lamb' (Part III, Movement 53). The limited use of the trumpets makes their inclusion in those few movements particularly effective.

In this chorus, Handel marked the entry of the trumpets as *da lontano e un poco piano*, meaning 'from a distance and somewhat quiet'. His original intention was to place the trumpets offstage at this point in order to intensify the effect of distance. Some modern performances of *Messiah* incorporate this practice, if the venue makes it easy to arrange.

The trumpets are not given a timpani accompaniment in this chorus, contrary to what might have been expected. The timpani are heard for the first time in the 'Hallelujah' Chorus – another example of leaving something in reserve for later in the oratorio.

Part I Scene 5: The Messiah's Ministry

18. **Air (soprano)**
Rejoice greatly, O daughter of Zion; shout, O daughter of Jerusalem: behold, thy King cometh unto thee. He is the righteous Saviour, and he shall speak peace unto the heathen. (Zechariah 9:9a, 10b)
19. **Recitative (contralto)**
Then shall the eyes of the blind be opened, and the ears of the deaf unstopped. Then shall the lame man leap as an hart, and the tongue of the dumb shall sing. (Isaiah 35:5–6a)
20. **Duet (contralto and soprano)**
He shall feed his flock like a shepherd; and he shall gather the lambs with his arm, and carry them in his bosom, and gently lead those that are with young. (Isaiah 40:11)
Come unto him, all ye that labour; come unto him ye that are heavy laden, and he will give you rest. Take his yoke upon you, and learn of him; for he is meek and lowly of heart, and ye shall find rest for your souls. (Matthew 11:28–29)
21. **Chorus**
His yoke is easy, his burthen is light. (Matthew 11:30)

Overview of the scene

Two surprises confront us in this scene, which is designed to cover the whole of Jesus' ministry up to the cross and resurrection.

The first surprise is the brevity of the scene. Clearly Jennens had in mind to take audiences as quickly as possible from Christmas to Good Friday, from the crib to the cross – and yet, at the same time, to provide a few selected verses which would accurately summarise the character and ministry of Jesus.

The other surprise is that, instead of going straight to the Gospels to find such material, Jennens turns first in the direction of the Old Testament and selects parts of some verses from Zechariah, a one-and-a-half verse section from Isaiah and another verse from Isaiah. Only then does he go to the Gospels, selecting three consecutive verses from the end of Matthew 11, including Jesus' invitation to *'come unto him'*.

This is Jennens at his best. He knew that he needed to keep things moving, so as to be able to provide a substantial section in Part II on the cross. His instinct was to focus on 'Jesus Christ and him crucified', to borrow the apostle Paul's phrase describing the focus of his own preaching (1 Cor 2:2). With his competent grasp of the big picture of the Old Testament, Jennens therefore painted a picture of Jesus' whole ministry with a few deft brushstrokes.

Two parallel themes link the Bible texts chosen for this scene.

The first theme is the caring compassion of Jesus the Messiah:

- Although Jennens omits the part of Zechariah 9:9 which describes the Messiah as 'humble' from Movement 18, this quality is implied in the phrase from verse 10, *'he shall speak peace unto the heathen'*.
- In Movement 19, we are shown his concern for the needy in Isaiah 35:5–6a.
- In the first part of Movement 20, we see his loving care as a shepherd in Isaiah 40:11.
- In the second part of Movement 20, where the selected text is Matthew 11:28–29, we find Jesus' description of himself as *'meek and lowly of heart'*.

The second theme (running in parallel to the first) concerns the various groups of disadvantaged and vulnerable in each of the Biblical texts:

- In Movement 18, the Messiah deals peacefully with *'the heathen'* – namely the nations or the Gentiles. Who would have expected outsiders to benefit from the Messiah's gracious rule?
- In Movement 19, we meet *'the 'blind', 'the deaf', 'the lame man'* and *'the dumb'*.

- In Movement 20, his care is shown to *'his flock'*, *'the lambs'* and *'those that are with young'*, and offered to *'all ye that labour ... that are heavy laden'*.

A few comments on how the three Old Testament sections that Jennens chooses connect with the New Testament may be helpful.

- Matthew and John see the fulfilment of the end of Zechariah 9:9 in Jesus' public entry into Jerusalem, seated on a donkey, on the day we call Palm Sunday (Matt 21:5; John 12:15), while Mark and Luke make the same connection more implicitly. However, presumably because Jennens does not wish to focus on the triumphal entry, the end part of verse 9 is among the parts of those two verses that he omits.
- Isaiah 35:5–6a is implicitly referred to by Jesus in Matthew 11:4b–5 (also Luke 7:22).
- Isaiah 40:11, speaking of the one who *'shall feed his flock like a shepherd'*, immediately summons up thoughts of Jesus' self-identification as the good shepherd of John 10.

Following those three Old Testament extracts, Jennens makes excellent use of a well-chosen New Testament text. He selects a three-verse section from Matthew 11:28–30 to give us what can best be described as the 'evangelistic appeal' of the oratorio. Just as every sermon needs to challenge the listener with an application (or challenge), the same can be said of the 'sermon' of Handel's *Messiah* – the application being 'Come to Jesus'.

If anyone objects that an evangelistic appeal should come at the very end of the work, the response can be made that the challenge is placed at the end of Part I, just before a break in the performance, in order to leave the audience in no doubt that they have not come merely to be entertained, but to be given a message of great importance, that should be taken to heart. Furthermore, the audience should be alerted by the invitation of those verses to take good note of the person and work of the Messiah to be presented in Parts II and III, which proclaim his death, resurrection and triumph. Jennens's intention at the very end of the oratorio (where we might have placed the challenge) is to sound a note of praise and adoration.

We turn now to a more detailed examination of the four short Bible passages used in this scene.

Zechariah 9:9–10 (The Saviour–King)

Movement 18 is an air with words from part of Zechariah 9:9–10, sung by the soprano. These two verses constitute a unit in themselves within the Book of Zechariah. They make up a twelve-line poem, and Jennens has used only five of those lines. In their entirety, the two verses read as follows in the ESV, with the lines retained by Jennens highlighted:

> **Rejoice greatly, O daughter of Zion!**
> **Shout aloud, O daughter of Jerusalem!**
> **behold, your king is coming to you;**
> **righteous and having salvation is he,**
> humble and mounted on a donkey,
> on a colt, the foal of a donkey.
>
> I will cut off the chariot from Ephraim
> and the war horse from Jerusalem;
> and the battle bow shall be cut off,
> **and he shall speak peace to the nations;**
> his rule shall be from sea to sea,
> and from the River to the ends of the earth.

The previous section (Zech 9:1–8) has the theme of war as God's judgement on his people's enemies. By contrast, in verses 9–10, we meet God's *'king'* who exercises a rule of peace on behalf of his people. This king is none other than the Messiah, and God announces his arrival. So the king is presented as a man, a human being – but a man who is closely associated with God. There are echoes here of other Old Testament messianic prophecies. One of these is Genesis 49:10–11 (already referred to in the Introduction), where Jacob, blessing his sons on his death-bed, foretells:

> The sceptre shall not depart from Judah,
> nor the ruler's staff from between his feet,
> until tribute comes to him,
> and to him shall be the obedience of the peoples.

Then comes a reference to this royal son of Judah 'binding his foal to the vine and his donkey's colt to the choice vine', which provides a verbal link with this passage from Zechariah.

Other examples of echoes of such messianic anticipations include Psalm 2, the archetypal messianic psalm (also mentioned in the Introduction), referring to God having set his 'king' on Zion his holy hill (Ps 2:6), and Psalm 72:8, referring to the 'king' in messianic terms: 'May he have dominion from sea to sea, and from the River to the ends of the earth.' This last phrase is deliberately quoted at the end of verse 10 of the Zechariah passage here. The two 'seas' are the Mediterranean and the Red Sea, and the 'River' is the Euphrates.

The two verses from Zechariah begin with a call to Zion/Jerusalem (standing for God's people) to rejoice exuberantly that their king is coming. The king's character is spelt out: he is *'righteous'* and the possessor of 'salvation' (a *'Saviour'* in the AV). Furthermore, he is 'humble', as indicated by his being 'mounted on a donkey', with the reference to the 'colt' being a parallelism, suggested no doubt by Genesis 49:11, already referred to. While it was not remarkable for a king or a prince to ride on a donkey rather than a horse, a donkey was an appropriate mount for one who came on a mission of peace.

Verse 10 has three lines dealing with the king's complete dismantling of all weaponry ('chariot', 'war horse', and 'battle bow'), followed by three lines about his coming kingdom. It will usher in peace for the world, including a reuniting of the northern and southern kingdoms, as indicated by the mention of 'Ephraim' and 'Jerusalem' in the first half of verse 10. As in the previous movement, we should understand this peace not only as the absence of the instruments of war but also the presence of everything good and wholesome that belongs to the Hebrew concept of *shalom*.

What should we make of Jennens's edited version of Zechariah 9:9–10? It is certainly instructive for the listener to be aware of the fuller picture to which the selected verses point. As already suggested, Jennens probably had no wish to single out the triumphal entry into Jerusalem in his brief summary of Christ's ministry – hence his omission of the last two lines of verse 9. The omission of five of the six lines of verse 10 can be defended on the grounds that it is not Jennens's purpose at this stage of the oratorio to highlight the Messiah's victorious rule over the nations, as that will be clearly presented towards the end of Part II. So the audience's focus in this movement is clearly directed to the joyful celebration of the coming of the perfect king who offers salvation and peace to all mankind.

Isaiah 35:5–6a (The healer of the deepest needs of mankind)

The next movement, Movement 19, is a recitative sung by the contralto, with the text being Isaiah 35:5–6a. It is a very brief movement (lasting only 28 seconds on my recording of *Messiah*) but the content of this short section is highly significant. Given that the other movements of this scene focus on the character of the Messiah, this is the only movement that focuses on the activity of Jesus during the three years leading up to the cross.

The text is Isaiah 35:5–6a, which forms the central, pivotal part of a poem which occupies the whole of Isaiah 35. The ESV gives the heading for this chapter 'The Ransomed Shall Return'. It is a marvellous passage of hope which deserves to be read in its entirety. The previous chapter consists of a promise of God's judgement on the nations, which is the necessary accompaniment to the promise of salvation for his people here in chapter 35: 'Behold, your God will come with vengeance, with the recompense of God. He will come and save you' (Isa 35:4).

The fulfilment of salvation is described in this chapter as living under God's rule and experiencing prosperity and blessing. Just as God had promised Abraham a people and a land (Gen 12:1–3), Isaiah describes the fulfilment of salvation with a focus on the land and God's people:

- The land will enjoy blessing: the desert will bloom (v 1–2) and it will be a place of fertility (v 6b–7) and security (v 9).
- God's people will be filled with joy: God will make a highway so that his people can travel to the land of blessing (v 8).

It will be evident that the prospect of a return from exile, which we met in Isaiah 40 in Scene 1, is anticipated in this earlier chapter of Isaiah. In addition, in the words of the verses included in this movement (v 5–6a), *'the blind'* will see, *'the deaf'* will hear, *'the lame man'* will leap, and *'the dumb'* will sing. Isaiah combines two faculties of perception (eyes and ears) and two of action (leaping and singing). These four transformations are a picture of redemption of the whole person.

Why did Jennens decide to make use of Isaiah 35:5–6a as the text to present Christ's ministry? Almost certainly it is because (as mentioned above) Isaiah 35:5–6a is implicitly referred to by Jesus in Matthew 11:4b–5 (also Luke 7:22): 'Go and tell John what you hear and see: the blind receive their sight and the lame walk, lepers are cleansed and the deaf hear, and the dead are raised up, and the poor have good news preached to them.'[1]

It will be helpful to examine that Gospel incident before returning to a further consideration of Isaiah 35. At this stage in the Gospel narrative John the Baptist, languishing in prison following his courageous denunciation of Herod Antipas's immoral union with his sister-in-law Herodias, sends a message through his disciples to ask Jesus, 'Are you the one who is to come, or shall we look for another?' (Matt 11:3). In other words, the question is: 'Are you the Messiah, or not?' It seems that, despite John the Baptist's earlier endorsement of Jesus as 'the one who is to come' (for example, John 3:25–30), John was now perplexed that Jesus had taken no action to deal with evil rulers such as Herod or the Romans. The fact that John himself was incarcerated and Jesus had done nothing to bring about his release meant that this was far more than an academic question!

John had spoken earlier of the Messiah's coming:

> He will baptise you with the Holy Spirit and fire. His winnowing fork is in his hand, and he will clear his threshing-floor and gather his wheat into the barn, but the chaff he will burn with unquenchable fire' (Matt 3:11b–12).

The Messiah would bring blessing (the Holy Spirit, and the wheat safely gathered in) and also judgement (fire, and the burning up of the chaff). So, John may have reasoned, if Jesus was the Messiah, was not his coming

[1] Jesus' words in that verse also echo Isaiah 61:1, and possibly also Isaiah 26:19 and 29:18–19.

supposed to usher in a 'day of vengeance' on God's enemies as well as an era of blessing on God's people (as in the discussion of Isaiah 34 and 35)?

It is instructive to notice that even an outstanding man of God such as John the Baptist, (whom Jesus would describe later in Matthew 11:11 as the greatest of all the prophets) could be plagued by doubts. But it is equally instructive to notice what he did with those doubts: he took them (via messengers) to the only one who could answer those doubts – namely Jesus.

John's mistake was to misunderstand the different purposes of Christ's two comings. As a prophet with all the outlook of the Old Testament, he saw the coming of the Messiah as a single event. But as we noted in the discussion at the beginning of Scene 2, the New Testament shows us a clearer perspective, with salvation and mercy belonging to the first coming, and judgement and vengeance belonging to the second.[2]

So Jesus' answer to John the Baptist (in Matthew 11:5) was that he should hold on to his conviction that he (Jesus) was indeed the Messiah, because he was clearly doing what the Messiah was anticipated to be doing. His miracles were to be understood as messianic signs. Luke, in his account of this incident, adds the following important comment between the question being asked and the answer being given: 'In that hour he healed many people of diseases and plagues and evil spirits, and on many who were blind he bestowed sight' (Luke 7:21).

We can see therefore that the link between Isaiah 35:5–6a and Jesus' words in Matthew 11:5 provided Jennens with an effective means of giving a concise summary of the whole of Jesus' ministry.

We return now to a few further comments about Isaiah 35:5–6. It is not difficult to find passages in the Gospels that show Jesus carrying out acts

---

[2] It may be significant that both of the principal passages from Isaiah, to which Jesus is alluding in Matthew 11:5 (Isa 35:5-6 and 61:1), have references to judgement in their immediate context: 'Behold, your God will come with *vengeance*' (Isa 35:4) and 'the day of *vengeance of our God*' (Isa 61:2) (my italics). Jesus' purpose seems to be to show John that the blessings promised for the end time have arrived, even though judgement is delayed. It is significant too that in Luke 4:18-19, where Jesus quotes specifically from Isaiah 61:1-2, he deliberately omits the words 'the day of vengeance of our God.' At his first coming his purpose was 'to proclaim the year of the Lord's favour.'

of healing on *'the blind', 'the deaf', 'the lame man'* and *'the dumb'.* But we need to ask: What was Jesus' purpose in performing these deeds? There is more than one answer to that question.

First, Jesus' healing miracles were acts of mercy and compassion, which reflect the character of the Messiah. As we have seen, this is a recurring theme in each of the movements that make up this scene.

Second, Jesus' healing ministry gives us today a window through which to glimpse something of the wonder of what it will be like one day to live under the rule of the messianic King, when 'he will wipe away every tear from their eyes, and death shall be no more, neither shall there be mourning, nor crying nor pain any more' (Rev 21:4). Jesus' miraculous deeds point us forward to the new heaven and the new earth, which can be described as 'paradise restored'.

Third, we should view Jesus' miracles as illustrations, or visual aids, of the transformative power of his grace at a deep spiritual level, and not merely physical. The good news concerning our Messiah, as Part II of the oratorio will explain in its own way, is that God 'sent his Son to be the propitiation for our sins' (1 John 4:10). The priority of Jesus in his ministry was to preach the gospel. For example, Mark encapsulates Jesus' message in the first words of Jesus that he records: 'The time is fulfilled, and the kingdom of God is at hand; repent and believe in the gospel' (Mark 1:15).

There is no contradiction between the healing and preaching roles of Jesus. Physical needs in the world today have, ultimately, a spiritual cause, namely the entry of sin into God's perfect world in the Garden in Genesis 3. It needs to be stated clearly, of course, that, while some physical problems may be the direct result of the sufferer's own sin, in general terms there is no direct correlation between specific sins and physical suffering. We are all sinners, living in a world which has been spoilt by the all-pervasive effects of sin, and as a human race we suffer those consequences, including disease and disability. So that is the context within which we are to see the healings that Jesus performed as illustrations of his grace and power to bring about a profound spiritual change for those who look to him.

A right reading of the Book of Isaiah should lead us to that understanding. We can examine this with reference to the four messianic signs of Isaiah 35:5–6a.

Who are the *'blind'*, who have their sight restored? Who are the *'deaf'*, who are made to hear? The clue is to be found in Isaiah 6:9–10 (in the famous chapter that records Isaiah's call to ministry as a prophet). In those verses we learn that these people are the ones whom God himself has made blind and deaf ('their ears heavy') and their hearts 'dull' (or 'fat') as judgement on them for their persistent sinfulness.

Who is the *'lame man'*, empowered to leap like a deer? The previous two verses of Isaiah 35 supply the clue. We read:

> Strengthen the weak hands,
> and make firm the feeble knees.
> Say to those who have an anxious heart,
> 'Be strong; fear not!
> Behold, your God will come with vengeance.'
> (Isa 35:3–4a)

The 'lame' are those who are fearful, inclined to disbelieve that God is able, let alone willing, to rescue them.

Who are the *'mute'*, given a voice to sing for joy? Here, we turn back to Isaiah 32:4: 'The heart of the hasty will understand and know, and the tongue of the stammerers will hasten to speak distinctly.' It would seem reasonable to see an equivalence between the two speech defects: the 'mute' of 35:6 and the 'stammerers' of 32:4. It is not physical ability that is lacking, but the will to speak the truth clearly.

So the transformation which is spoken of in Isaiah 35:5–6a is a profoundly spiritual and moral one, and similar comments could be made about the other categories of sufferers referred to in other similar passages of Isaiah (for example, the poor, the captives, the bound, the dead – and the lepers, whom Jesus includes in his words in Matthew 11:5).[3] All these terms point to spiritual conditions, which represent variations on the theme of lives disordered as the result of sin. The truth is expressed in pictorial terms as

[3] As mentioned in an earlier footnote, those other passages are Isaiah 61:1, and also Isaiah 26:19 and 29:18-19.

those with physical needs, but the reality is a deeper problem of the soul. So when Jesus comes and shows his grace and power to deal with such physical needs in his ministry, the truth which is being proclaimed is that he is the Saviour who deals with mankind's real and underlying problem: he calls people to repentance, he forgives sins, and he restores men and women to a relationship with God.

This has been a substantial discussion of Isaiah 35:5–6a, but it should demonstrate for us very clearly that Jennens's choice of these one-and-a half Old Testament verses as the summary of the whole of Jesus' ministry was an amazingly skilful one. This short Old Testament text is a key that unlocks a door into understanding such a wealth of Bible truth.

So far in this scene we have explored two of its three short Old Testament passages. But already we can see that the identikit of Jesus the Messiah being compiled for us by Jennens is unmistakably that of a perfect king, who brings a message of peace and salvation, performs deeds of transforming mercy and grace, and gives assurance of the blessings which his people will one day enjoy in full measure.

Isaiah 40:11 (The caring shepherd)

The next two movements belong together, combining texts from Isaiah 40 and Matthew 11, and they bring Part I of the oratorio to its conclusion. Movement 20 consists of an air in two stanzas. The first half of it is a setting of Isaiah 40:11, sung by the contralto, and the second half is a setting of Matthew 11:28–29. Movement 21 is a chorus, the earlier part largely in contrapuntal style and moving into block chord style in its final stages. It is closely linked with the second half of the previous air, being a setting of the very next verse, Matthew 11:30.

It is possible that Jennens was drawn to Isaiah 40:11 by his earlier use of verses from that chapter of Isaiah in Scenes 1 and 3 and because this verse's description of the Messiah as a caring shepherd follow on most appropriately from the Messiah's qualities highlighted in Zechariah 9:9–10 and Isaiah 35:5–6a.

We can tease out a further pair of thematic links in the oratorio, which are introduced at this point.

The first has to do with the depiction of mankind:

- In Movement 20, men and women are the sheep, or *'flock'*, of whom the Messiah takes care.
- In Movement 26 (in Part II), they are foolish sheep who have *'gone astray'*.

The second, and parallel, thematic link concerns the depiction of Jesus the Messiah, in terms drawn from the world of sheep:

- In Movement 20, he is the shepherd of his flock.
- In Movement 22 (at the beginning of Part II), he is *'the Lamb of God, that taketh away the sin of the world.'*
- In Movement 53 (almost at the end of Part III), he is the victorious *'Lamb that was slain'* and is now worthy to receive all glory (Movement 53).

The implicit truth in these parallel progressions is that the Messiah, who is the shepherd, is to take the place of the sheep and is slain for them – an apparent defeat which turns out to be a glorious victory. But this discussion anticipates the subject matter of the opening scene of Part II.

Isaiah 40:10–11 forms a marvellously balanced pair of verses in this purple passage of Scripture. Verse 10 tells us, 'Behold, the Lord God comes with might, and his arm rules for him.' But in verse 11, his *'arm'* is mentioned again, this time in terms of the loving arms in which *'he shall gather the lambs'*.

It is God himself who is described in these two verses as sovereign and shepherd. He is the shepherd who shall *'feed'* and *'gather'* and *'carry'* and *'lead'* his sheep. As indicated a little earlier, we should take Isaiah 40:11 as an anticipation of Jesus' own description of himself in John 10 as 'the good shepherd', who not only knows his sheep, but also lays down his life for them (John 10:11 and 15) – again the cross is in view.

Matthew 11:28–30 (The burden-bearer and teacher)

The second half of Movement 20, with Matthew 11:28–29 as its text, provides what has been described earlier as the oratorio's evangelistic appeal. And, as noted earlier, the opening words of verse 28 are changed from the first to the third person in the interests of due reverence: *'Come unto him.'*

In the 'Overview of the scene' (above) we noted a particular thematic link in this scene, namely the focus of the Messiah's humble, gentle ministry to those who are disadvantaged and vulnerable. In this movement, this care is offered to *'all ye that labour ... that are heavy laden'*.

Jesus issues two invitations in verses 28 and 29.

The first invitation is to come to him, and he will give *'rest'*. We, to whom this invitation comes, are pictured as oxen, crushed by a heavy load. While the burdens that men and women carry along life's journey are many and varied, the particular one in view must be the burden of guilt and sin. Jesus can promise *'rest'* to those who know the heavy weight of a guilty conscience, because he is the burden-bearer.

An apt illustration of the release from the burden of sin comes in John Bunyan's 'Pilgrim's Progress', when Christian, with his heavy load on his back, comes to the cross:

> So I saw in my dream, that just as Christian came up with the cross, his burden loosed from off his shoulders and fell from off his back, and began to tumble, and so continued to do, till it came to the mouth of the sepulchre, where it fell in, and I saw it no more. Then was Christian glad and lightsome, and said, with a merry heart, 'He hath given me rest by his sorrow, and life by his death.' ...Then Christian gave three leaps for joy.[4]

As the old chorus puts it, 'Burdens are lifted at Calvary.'[5]

The second invitation is in verse 29: 'Take my yoke upon you, and learn from me, for I am gentle and lowly in heart, and you will find rest for your souls.'

---

[4] J. Bunyan, *Pilgrim's Progress* (London: J.M. Dent & Sons Ltd, 1907), 42–43.
[5] *Burdens Are Lifted at Calvary,* words and music J.M. Moore – Youth Praise (London: Falcon, 1966).

There is a beautiful balance between these two invitations. First, he takes our yoke, which is the burden crushing us. Then he places his yoke on us. Clearly these are not two alternative invitations: to accept the one is at the same time to accept the other. To come to Jesus is to take his yoke upon us. And we notice that both invitations are coupled with a promise of rest – verse 28: 'and I will give you rest'; verse 29: 'and you will find rest for your souls'.

The picture continues, as in verse 28, to be that of oxen, but here it is a team, or pair, of oxen pulling the plough or cart. The farmer has put together an older, experienced ox, and a young inexperienced ox, so that the younger can learn from the older. In that picture, we are to be the younger, inexperienced ox, and our team-mate – the experienced, wise one from whom we are to learn – is Jesus. The yoke in verse 29 is a symbol for submission to authority, because the truth is that Jesus the Messiah is to be not only our Saviour, who releases the sinner from guilt, but the Lord and Master, who teaches and trains those who become his disciples.

Jesus' qualification to be the perfect giver of rest is that he is *'meek and lowly of heart'*, or 'gentle and lowly in heart' (ESV). It would be wrong to fall into the trap of regarding 'gentleness' or 'meekness' as a sign of weakness. While it is correct to dismiss the old Sunday School pictures of an effeminate Jesus, the word 'meekness', rightly understood, conveys the idea of strength under control. Moses is described as 'very meek, more than all people who were on the face of the earth' (Num 12:3), but no one could accuse Moses of being weak. Nor can that accusation be levelled against Jesus, whose authority was plain to friend and foe alike. Rather, we are assured that in Jesus we find someone who supremely understands our weaknesses and needs and therefore deals with us with complete and insightful tenderness.

Movement 21, a chorus, carries the text of the very next verse: Matthew 11:30. Here is the answer to the unspoken question: Is there a catch? Will this yoke that Jesus gives prove to be another heavy burden, as bad as or even worse than the previous one? The answer is: 'For my yoke is easy, and my burden is light.'[6] For a yoke to be easy, it has to fit smoothly and comfortably. Jesus is the master-carpenter, and his yokes fit well. Nor do

---

[6] The text of the oratorio uses the word 'burthen', which is an archaic form of the word 'burden.'

we need to imagine the Christian life as one of drudgery. The apostle John reinforces the assurance that Christ's burden is light when he writes about obedience to God's commandments being one of the hallmarks of a genuine believer: 'And his commandments are not burdensome' (1 John 5:3). Augustine wrote that God is the master 'whom to serve is perfect freedom'.[7] Thomas Cranmer incorporated this phrase in one of the Morning Prayer collects in the *Book of Common Prayer*.

What to listen out for in the music in Part I Scene 5

18. Air: *'Rejoice greatly, O daughter of Zion'*

This movement is a virtuoso *coloratura* air, designed for the soprano soloist to sing an item that expresses great joy with musical embellishments.

An upward fourth followed by a rest (another example of the unifying motif, mentioned earlier) accents *'Rejoice'* at the beginning of the initial phrase and further repeats of this word are rendered as seemingly endless *coloraturas*.

The first statement of *'Behold, thy King cometh unto thee'* is given dotted rhythm, suggesting stateliness.

The middle section announces, in mellow mood, that *'he is the righteous Saviour, and he shall speak peace unto the heathen'*, with *'peace'* repeated several times as a long note.

Finally, a *da capo* seems to begin, but only the first entry of the voice is exactly the same, followed by even more varied *coloraturas* and embellishments to end the air.

19. Recitative: *'Then shall the eyes of the blind be opened'*

To reinforce the comments above about the one-and-a-half Bible verses that make up this item, the brevity of this recitative should not be allowed to detract from us taking on board the full weight of the significance of the Messiah's ministry.

[7] F. Colquhoun (ed.), *Parish Prayers* (London: Hodder and Stoughton, 1967), 382.

20. Duet: *'He shall feed his flock like a shepherd'*

The contralto sings the first stanza in the key of F major, and the soprano the second stanza in the closely related key of Bb major. Not only are the keys chosen appropriately for the range of the respective voices, but also the change of key, up a fourth (and we should note here another instance of the recurring upward fourth motif), provides what might be described as a 'lift', not just literally but emotionally as well.

The melody for both stanzas is sung in 12/8 time and is reminiscent of the 'Pastoral Symphony' (Movement 13), but by contrast to that earlier item where it moved first up and then down, this time it moves first down and then up.

21. Chorus: *'His yoke is easy'*

The theme of the fugue is light and easy-going, to match the theme of the words. *'His yoke'* is set as yet another upward fourth, and *'easy'* is a playful *coloratura.*

The texture is intensified to the end, when all proclaim as a solemn statement, with the tempo slowed down, *'and his burthen is light'.*

Part II: From the cross to glory

PART II SCENE I: THE MESSIAH'S SUFFERINGS

22. **Chorus**
Behold the Lamb of God, that taketh away the sin of the world. (John 1:29b)

23. **Air**
He was despised and rejected of men, a man of sorrows and acquainted with grief. (Isaiah 53:3a)
He gave his back to the smiters, and his cheeks to them that plucked off the hair: he hid not his face from shame and spitting. (Isaiah 50:6)

24. **Chorus**
Surely he hath borne our griefs and carried our sorrows; he was wounded for our transgressions, he was bruised for our iniquities: the chastisement of our peace was upon him. (Isaiah 53:4–5c)

25. **Chorus**
And with his stripes we are healed. (Isaiah 53:5d)

26. **Chorus**
All we like sheep have gone astray, we have turned every one to his own way; and the Lord hath laid on him the iniquity of us all. (Isaiah 53:6)

27. ***Accompagnato* (tenor)**
All they that see him laugh him to scorn: they shoot out their lips, and shake their heads, saying: (Psalm 22:7)

28. **Chorus**
He trusted in God that he would deliver him: let him deliver him, if he delight in him. (Psalm 22:8)

29. ***Accompagnato* (tenor)**
Thy rebuke hath broken his heart; he is full of heaviness; he looked for some to have pity on him, but there was no man, neither found he any to comfort him. (Psalm 69:20)

30. ***Arioso* (tenor)**
Behold, and see if there be any sorrow like unto his sorrow! (Lamentations 1:12b)

Introduction to Part II

The length of the opening scene of Part II (consisting of five choruses, an air, an *arioso* and two *accompagnatos*) – longer than any other scene – seems to indicate clearly that Jennens intended this section of the work, focusing on the sufferings of the Messiah, to be the centrepiece of the oratorio.

A comment needs to be made about the remarkable use of predominantly Old Testament material in Part II. With the exception of the very first and very last movement of Part II ('Behold the Lamb of God' and the 'Hallelujah' Chorus), every movement in Part II is a setting of an Old Testament text or of a New Testament verse which quotes from the Old Testament. In view of the subject matter, we might have expected more New Testament material. This is in no way intended as a criticism but rather as a tribute to Jennens's grasp of the Christ-centredness of the whole of Scripture.

The Lamb of God of John 1:29

The text of Movement 22, the chorus *'Behold the Lamb of God'*, consists of the words of John the Baptist in John 1:29. In this movement, Jennens uses material from the Gospels for only the fourth (and final) time – the earlier Gospel passages being Matthew 1:23 (Movement 8), Luke 2:8–11, 13–14 (in Movements 14–17) and Matthew 11:28–30 (in Movements 20b–21).

The thoughtful listener will hear the echo of the earlier reference to John the Baptist towards the beginning of Part I: 'the voice' crying in the wilderness (Isa 40:3, Movement 2). The thematic balance between the beginnings of both Part I and Part II is a masterful touch on Jennens's part. John the Baptist points to the coming of the Messiah as the deliverer (Part I), and he points to the coming of the Messiah as the sacrificial Lamb of God (Part II). These two roles in no way conflict with each other; on the contrary, it is by dying as the sacrificial Lamb that the Messiah proves to be the mighty deliverer.

The phrase *'the Lamb of God'* is rich in Old Testament allusions. Throughout the Old Testament era lambs were sacrificial animals (the earliest example being Abel's offering in Genesis 4:4). But particular instances stand out as having special significance. There is the lamb (or ram) provided by God for Abraham, to be sacrificed in place of Isaac (Gen 22:8, 13). There is the Passover lamb of Exodus 12, whose blood – daubed on the lintels and doorposts of Hebrew households – saved God's people from judgement. Most significantly in the context of the oratorio, there is the lamb of Isaiah 53, who was led to the slaughter for the sins of God's people. Five of the movements that follow (23–26 and 31) use texts from Isaiah 53.

The truth that Jesus is *'the Lamb of God'*, provided by God himself, underlines the sobering reality that we are utterly unable to provide for our own atonement. Our salvation is the free gift of God.

The significance of the sacrificial *'Lamb of God'* is that he *'taketh away'* sin. While all animals sacrificed in temple worship were regarded as a substitute for the worshipper (in other words, dying the death that the worshipper deserved) and therefore 'taking away' the individual's sin, there was a particularly significant symbolism from the annual Day of Atonement (in Leviticus 16) involving the so-called 'scapegoat' (admittedly a goat, rather than a lamb): instead of the animal being sacrificed, the high priest laid his hands on its head, thus transferring on to it the guilt of the people, and then it was released in the wilderness as a representation of the people's sin being taken away.

We should notice the scope of the Lamb's achievement: dealing with *'the sin of the world'*. Every kind of sin and evil is covered, and by implication this offer of forgiveness embraces people from all nations: Jews and Gentiles.

Understanding the implications of this great Bible truth played a major part in the conversion of Charles Simeon, who became an influential evangelical leader in the late eighteenth and early nineteenth century and exercised a powerful ministry at Holy Trinity Church Cambridge for many years. In his *Memoir* he relates that shortly after his arrival as an undergraduate at King's College Cambridge, he was informed that he was obliged by a college rule to take Holy Communion in the College Chapel within three weeks. What happened next is told in his own words:

> 'What', said I, '**must** I attend?' On being informed that I must, the thought rushed into my mind that Satan

> himself was as fit to attend as I; and that if I must attend, I must **prepare** for my attendance there.[1]

He read religious books and was in great distress of mind, knowing that he would have to take the Lord's Supper again on Easter Sunday. His story continues:

> But in Passion Week, as I was reading Bishop Wilson on the Lord's Supper, I met with an expression to this effect – 'that the Jews knew what they did, when they transferred their sin to the head of their offering.' The thought came into my mind, What, may I transfer all my guilt to another? Has God provided an Offering for me, that I may lay my sins on His head? Then, God willing, I will not bear them on my own soul one moment longer. Accordingly I sought to lay my sins upon the sacred head of Jesus; and on the Wednesday began to have a hope of mercy; on the Thursday that hope increased; on the Friday and Saturday it became more strong; and on the Sunday morning, Easter-day, April 4, I awoke early with those words upon my heart and lips, 'Jesus Christ is risen today! Hallelujah! Hallelujah! Hallelujah!' From that hour peace flowed in rich abundance into my soul; and at the Lord's Table in our Chapel I had the sweetest access to God through my blessed Saviour.[2]

The Suffering Servant of Isaiah 53

Isaiah 53 represents the Old Testament chapter *par excellence* outlining the Christian understanding of penal substitution – in other words, the Bible's teaching that, when Jesus died on the cross, he was standing in as our substitute and bearing in full measure the wrath (or judgement, or punishment) of God that our sin deserved. As we shall see in the following pages, Isaiah 53 states the truth of Christ's penal substitution no less clearly than the teaching of the New Testament, as for example in

---

[1] H. C. G. Moule, *Charles Simeon* (London: The Inter-Varsity Fellowship, 1965), 24–26.

[2] Moule, *Charles Simeon*, 24–26.

1 Peter 3:18a: 'For Christ also suffered once for sins, the righteous for the unrighteous, that he might bring us to God' – where the words 'for the unrighteous' in this verse mean 'instead of the unrighteous.'

Isaiah 53 is referred to, or quoted, a number of times in the New Testament. One particular instance is Acts 8:32–33 (quoting Isaiah 53:7–8) – the context of this passage being the meeting of Philip with the Ethiopian eunuch, who was reading from Isaiah 53 while travelling in his chariot and was puzzled by the reference to an individual who 'like a sheep ... was led to the slaughter.' The man asked, 'About whom, I ask you, does the prophet say this, about himself or about someone else?' (Acts 8:34). Then we are told: 'Philip opened his mouth, and beginning with this Scripture he told him the good news about Jesus' (Acts 8:35). It is not at all fanciful to suggest that the apostle Peter had Isaiah 53 in mind when he wrote about the purpose of Jesus' death in the verse quoted in the previous paragraph, particularly as the closing verses of chapter 2 of his first letter draw heavily on phrases from that chapter of Isaiah (1 Peter 2:22–25).

Of the many illustrations of penal substitution, one of the clearest is the incident in C S Lewis's *The Lion, the Witch and the Wardrobe*, when the Witch demands the right to kill Edmund because of his treachery against Aslan. She invokes the law, referred to in the book as the 'Deep Magic' which the Emperor put into Narnia from the beginning, in order to support her demand. The only way for Edmund to be delivered from his doom is for Aslan to take Edmund's place and allow himself to take Edmund's place and to be humiliated, mocked, shaved and killed on the Stone Table.[3] In a very similar way sinful human beings stand condemned by God's holy law as rebels against him. They can only be delivered by the substitutionary death of the Lord Jesus Christ who, in the words of the *Book of Common Prayer* Holy Communion Service, on the cross 'made ... (by his one oblation of himself once offered) a full, perfect, and sufficient sacrifice, oblation, and satisfaction, for the sins of the whole

[3] C. S. Lewis, *The Lion, the Witch and the Wardrobe* (Harmondsworth: Penguin Books, 1959), chapters 13-14.

world.'[4] What happens next in the C S Lewis story will be told later at the appropriate point!

Within the Book of Isaiah, 52:13–53:12 forms what is often called the fourth Servant Song.[5] This is one of the instances in the Bible where the chapter division has been placed wrongly, so that when reference is made to 'Isaiah 53' this is often shorthand for the whole section including the last three verses of the previous chapter.

A figure emerges in the later chapters of Isaiah who is called 'the servant' – but who is this individual? Elsewhere in the Old Testament, God's covenant people Israel had been described as God's 'servant', but Israel is now disqualified from this role, since the nation has given itself up to idolatry and is blind and deaf: 'Who is blind but my servant, or deaf as my messenger whom I send? Who is blind as my dedicated one, or blind as the servant of the Lord?' (Isa 42:19). The earlier discussion, in the section on Isaiah 35:5–6 (Movement 19), mentioned the moral and spiritual significance in the Book of Isaiah attaches to such terms as 'blind' and 'deaf.' So this means that Israel is unfit for the role, but God declares that he will raise up a servant who will declare his mind to the nations and bring justice to the earth. Who, then, is this servant to be? Isaiah 49:3 gives this answer: 'You are my servant, Israel, in whom I will be glorified.' The Lord announces to this servant, 'I will make you as a light for the nations, that my salvation may reach to the end of the earth' (Isa 49:6).

The answer to the question of the servant's identity appears to be contradictory. On the one hand, it is *not* Israel, because Israel is spiritually blind and deaf. On the other hand, it *is* Israel. How is the mystery to be solved? The answer is: the servant is one who is at the same time both *distinct from* sinful Israel and at the same time so closely *identified with* God's people that he can truly be said to represent them and in that sense 'be' Israel. In this fourth Servant Song of Isaiah 53, his identification with his people is so deep that he suffers for them in their place and himself pays the penalty of their sin.

One further point concerning this servant needs to be made. There was no understanding, generally speaking, in Old Testament times (and

[4] The Order for the Administration of the Lord's Supper or Holy Communion, *Book of Common Prayer,* 1662.

[5] The four Servant Songs occupy Isaiah 42:1-9; 49:1-6; 50:4-9; 52:13 – 53:12.

indeed up to the death and resurrection of Jesus and the Day of Pentecost), that this servant figure of Isaiah was the Messiah. That accounts for the perplexed question of the Ethiopian eunuch in Acts 8. The Messiah's role was understood as that of the conquering King, not of a sacrificial victim who was despised and rejected. Only in the light of the New Testament are we enabled to recognise that Jesus, in being 'lifted up' in the sense of being crucified, was at the same time being 'lifted up' in the sense of being exalted (John 12:32), so that the inscription placed by Pilate on the cross rightly ascribed to Jesus the title 'the King of the Jews' (John 19:19–22). However, for those who look on these events without the eyes of faith, the message of a crucified Messiah is folly and a scandal (1 Cor 1:23).

The fourth Servant Song (Isa 52:13–53:12) is a poem consisting of five stanzas. Charles Jennens's libretto for this scene makes use of the last verse of the second stanza (53:3) and most of the third stanza (53:4–6). He returns to another verse (53:8) in the next scene.

The Man of Sorrows of Isaiah 53:3

Movement 23 is an air for the contralto and begins with the first half of Isaiah 53:3. Jennens appropriately changes the AV's present tense 'is despised and rejected' to the past tense *'was despised and rejected'*. The word *'despised'* is used twice in the Bible text of this verse. Throughout Jesus' ministry we see him being despised and rejected. The apostle John announces this theme in the prologue to his Gospel: 'He was in the world, and the world was made through him, and yet the world did not know him. He came to his own, and his own people did not receive him' (John 1:10–11). Nathanael, later in the same chapter, dismisses the Jesus whom he has not yet met: 'Can anything good come out of Nazareth?' (John 1:46). But his rejection is most clearly seen in the events leading to the crucifixion, and a Holy Week prayer by J W G Masterton begins: 'Lord Jesus Christ, betrayed for thirty pieces of silver, deserted by your disciples, denied by Peter, mocked by Herod, scourged by Pilate, crowned with thorns, and nailed to the cross.'[6]

---

[6] F. Colquhoun (ed.), *Contemporary Parish Prayers* (London: Hodder and Stoughton, 1975), 41.

'A man of sorrows and acquainted with grief.' Christ's *'sorrows'* and *'grief'* referred to in this verse are unexplained at this point: it is the next verse (used in Movement 24) that reveals that they are our sorrows and grief which he has taken upon himself as his own. The phrase *'man of sorrows'* is the starting point of the well-known Good Friday hymn by Philip Bliss:[7]

> 'Man of Sorrows!' what a name
> For the Son of God, who came
> Ruined sinners to reclaim!
> Hallelujah! what a Saviour!

The Sufferer of Isaiah 50:6

The central section of this movement (Movement 23) includes a setting of Isaiah 50:6 (from the third Servant Song), a verse which prophetically focuses on aspects of Jesus' ordeal prior to crucifixion. *'He gave his back to the smiters'* is a description of the vicious and barbaric flogging that Jesus received (Matt 27:26); *'and his cheeks to them that plucked off the hair'* speaks of painful torture (Matt 27:30); *'shame and spitting'* reflects further aspects of the humiliation that Jesus received from Roman soldiers, spectators and senior clerics (Matt 27:29–30, 39–44).

The Suffering Servant of Isaiah 53:4–6

Movements 24, 25 and 26 are all choruses and they take us through the third (and central) stanza of the fourth Servant Song (Isa 53:4–6, but omitting the second half of verse 4). These verses are intensely personal in a collective way. The pronoun 'we', together with 'us' and 'our', occurs most frequently in this stanza – ten times in all. The words represent the insightful understanding, on the part of the amazed people of God, of the deep significance of the servant's substitutionary sacrifice. It is therefore highly appropriate that these words should be sung by the choir rather than one of the four soloists.

In my opinion, Movement 24 is possibly the most moving of all items in the oratorio, and a musical comment on this chorus and the two that follow it will be included below. 'We', together with its related forms, is

[7] Philip Bliss, 'Man of Sorrows', in *Communion Songs* (1857).

not the only recurring pronoun here. In fact, these verses focus our attention on a contrast between 'he' and 'we.' *'He hath borne our griefs and carried our sorrows'* draws its imagery from the ritual concerning the scapegoat on the Day of Atonement in Leviticus 16. Everything that blights and spoils our lives – *'our griefs',* or infirmities, and *'our sorrow'* has been *'borne'* (lifted as a burden) and *'carried'* (shouldered) by him.

Further comments on Movement 24 will follow after the next section, which examines the use of Isaiah 53:4 in Matthew 8:17.

A brief look at Matthew 8:17

The context of Isaiah 53 and the references to this chapter in the rest of the Bible make it abundantly clear that the word 'infirmities' (the literal meaning of *'griefs'* in verse 4) is to be understood in a spiritual sense: on the cross Jesus was bearing our spiritual sickness upon himself. But Matthew 8:17 appears at first sight to be an exception to this consensus. In a short paragraph (Matt 8:14–17), Matthew reports Jesus' healing of Peter's mother-in-law, of many demon-oppressed people and of those who were sick. Then he adds the comment: 'This was to fulfil what was spoken by the prophet Isaiah: "He took our illnesses and bore our diseases"' (Matt 8:17). This seems to be Matthew's own translation of the Hebrew. Instead of telling us that Jesus fulfilled Isaiah 53 by his sin-bearing on the cross, Matthew appears to be telling us that Jesus fulfilled this prophecy by his healing ministry.

The use of the word 'appears' in the previous sentence is deliberate, because in fact there is a deeply significant connection between both aspects of Jesus' ministry. The Bible consistently teaches that all sickness is caused, directly or indirectly, by sin. We touched on this whole area in the earlier comments on Isaiah 35:5–6 in the discussion of Movement 19. Sickness and death reflect the fact that here on earth we live with the consequences of the Fall. We still await the new heaven and the new earth, when 'he will wipe away every tear from their eyes, and death shall be no more, nor shall there be mourning nor crying nor pain any more' (Rev 21:4).

Matthew is well aware that Jesus came to save his people from their sins (Matt 1:21). He shows us Jesus demonstrating the priority of his ministry when he declares a paralysed man forgiven, before healing him physically, as proof that 'the Son of Man has authority on earth to forgive sins' (Matt 9:1–8). Also Matthew records Jesus' statement that his followers must adopt the pattern of servanthood, 'even as the Son of man came not to be served but to serve, and to give his life as a ransom for many' (Matt 20:28). This verse is particularly significant in that it is clearly a reference to Jesus' consciousness of his role as the suffering servant of Isaiah 53.

So why does Matthew 8:17 draw the connection between Isaiah 53 and Jesus' healing ministry? The simple answer, and one that is easily overlooked, is that in Matthew 8 we see Jesus' ministry before the cross. Matthew's Gospel, just like the other three Gospels, explains that it is on the cross, by his death, that Jesus would deal with the root problem of sin. His atoning sacrifice alone could be the means of ultimately remedying all the ills that result from the curse of sin on the human race, not least physical sickness. But in Matthew 8:17, we see first of all that Jesus identifies with men and women who are ravaged by the consequences of the Fall and, in anticipation of what he would achieve on the cross, takes people's infirmities on himself. Also, in the same way as was noted in the previous scene (in connection with Isaiah 35:5–6a), we are given here a glimpse of life without pain and disease in the new heaven and the new earth, which his saving death will bring about and which belongs to eternity to come. The atoning work of the Lord Jesus Christ achieves total redemption: of body as well as of soul – but this is the completeness of our salvation which belongs to the 'not yet' and which we still await.[8]

Isaiah 53:4–6 (again)

Jennens omits the second half of verse 4 of Isaiah 53, which for completeness we add in here: 'yet we esteemed him stricken, smitten by God, and afflicted.' The *'griefs'* and *'sorrows'* of the suffering servant were mentioned in verse 3 (Movement 23), and the onlookers acknowledge now that they misunderstood the situation. In verse 3, they wrongly thought that his sufferings originated from his own person, and as a result the servant was 'despised, and we esteemed him not.' In verse 4 they admit that they wrongly 'esteemed' him as deserving the punishment he was receiving as one 'smitten by God.'

[8] See, for example, Phil 3:20; 1 Pet 1:3-5.

The chorus of Movement 24 (to which we now return) takes us from the first part of verse 4 into verse 5 of Isaiah 53, carrying us to the heart of the matter as it moves beyond the sorrows and the grief to the sin which is their root cause. The problem is *'our transgressions'* and *'our iniquities'* – the former word indicating our acts of wilful rebellion, the latter the 'bentness' of our fallen human nature. 'He' is again emphatic in this verse: it is he (the servant) and none other who was *'wounded'* (or pierced) and *'bruised'* (or crushed) in our place. The *'chastisement'* that should have fallen on us fell on him and, amazingly, secures *'peace'* with God for 'us.'

The chorus of Movement 25 concludes Isaiah 53:5: *'And with his stripes we are healed.' 'Stripes',* or 'wounds' (NIV), refer to open, untreated lacerations. It is a striking word, especially as it is *'his stripes'* which are the means which brings about the healing of our wounds. As we noted a little earlier, this is not the alleviation of physical illnesses or emotional pain, but the forgiveness that God pours into broken lives as he binds up our spiritual wounds.

The chorus of Movement 26 is a setting of the text of the next verse, Isaiah 53:6. There is a change of subject. Instead of telling us what he (the servant) has done, this verse speaks of what we have done. There is a note of deep penitence here, with no hiding the folly and thoughtlessness of sin (*'All we like sheep have gone astray'*). Nor is there any hiding of the culpability of mankind (*'we have turned every one to his own way'*). The wonder is that *'the Lord hath laid on him the iniquity of us all.'*

The great Bible truth of penal substitutionary atonement is declared throughout Isaiah 53:4–6. We have sinned, but he has been punished. He was pierced and wounded, but we have been healed and forgiven. That truth is particularly spelt out in unmistakable clarity at the end of verse 6, with the Lord laying our sin (the sum total of the wickedness and rebellion of those he purposes to save) on him, the one substitutionary victim. *'All we'* (at the beginning of the verse) have sinned: on him has been laid the iniquity of *'us all'* (at the end of the verse).

On the cross, Jesus took on himself the curse of sin which, since the Fall in Genesis 3, has alienated mankind from God and in his own person he bore the full measure of God's righteous wrath which sin deserves. This is the reason for Christ's words on the cross, often referred to as the 'cry of dereliction': 'My God, my God, why have you forsaken me?' (Matt

27:46). With these words Jesus was deliberately quoting Psalm 22:1 (and did so in his native Aramaic), because on the cross he was fulfilling all that that remarkable psalm foretold, and it is for this reason that Jesus' words are expressed as a question. On the cross, Jesus, who from all eternity enjoyed intimate fellowship with the Father, was abandoned by the Father, so that we might never be abandoned; he who knew no sin was made sin for our sake (2 Cor 5:21). Here is how Martin Luther expressed this truth, in almost shocking terms, in his commentary on Galatians:

> Our most merciful Father, seeing us to be oppressed and overwhelmed with the curse of the law, and that we could never be delivered from it of our own power, sent his only Son into the world and laid upon him all the sins of all men, saying, Be thou Peter that denier, Paul that persecutor, David the adulterer, that sinner who did eat the fruit in Eden, that thief who hanged upon the cross, and be thou that person who has committed the sins of all men: see therefore that thou pay and satisfy for them.'[9]

The sufferer of Psalm 22:7–8

Movement 27 (a tenor *accompagnato*) and Movement 28 (a chorus) take us into Psalm 22 verses 7–8.[10] In the preceding section, verse 1 of this psalm was quoted (words which Jesus himself cried out on the cross). In a remarkable way, and in so much detail, Psalm 22 anticipates the crucifixion of Jesus. Readers would do well to turn to this psalm in its entirety.

As always happens when we consider the cross of Christ, we are compelled to see ourselves in the light of the unfolding events, and in this process we are helped by the chorus of Movement 28. Just as the earlier

---

[9] M. Luther, *Commentary on the Epistle to the Galatians* (London: James Clarke, 1953), 272.

[10] As happens elsewhere in 'Messiah', the first person statement of verse 7 is put into the third person. This quotation from the Book of Psalms unusually comes from the AV rather than from the *Book of Common Prayer*. Jennens takes the phrase *'if he delights in him'* from a marginal variant of the AV.

chorus of Movement 26 encouraged us to view ourselves as the sheep who have gone astray and the ones whose sin has been laid on the spotless Lamb of God, now in this movement we are invited to see ourselves as members of the crowd of ordinary passers-by who were responsible for the death of Jesus and approved of it just as if we had been there. One of a number of hymns that pick up on this motif is one by Horatius Bonar, which includes these words:

> 'Twas I that shed the sacred blood;
> I nailed Him to the tree;
> I crucified the Christ of God;
> I joined the mockery.
>
> And of that shouting multitude
> I feel that I am one;
> And in that din of voices rude
> I recognize my own.
>
> Around yon cross the throng I see,
> Mocking the Sufferer's groan;
> Yet still my voice it seems to be,
> As if I mocked alone.[11]

Jennens may well have selected these particular verses from the psalm because Matthew deliberately, but implicitly, shows them being fulfilled as Jesus hung on the cross. Matthew 27:39 reads: 'And those who passed by derided him, wagging their heads'. In the same chapter, verse 43 records the mocking words of the chief priests, with the scribes and elders: 'He trusts in God; let God deliver him now, if he desires him. For he said, "I am the Son of God."'

We read those same details, almost in their entirety, in Psalm 22:7–8, just as if Jesus himself on the cross were in a position to dictate the words in the midst of his agony. The mockers' taunts in verse 8 are a mixture of unintended truth and of woeful error. The truth is that Jesus' claim to be the 'Son of God' was a claim to messiahship and that Jesus did indeed trust in God – in their hypocritical malice they could never have recognised the completeness of the Son's faithful submission to the

[11] Horatius Bonar, 'I see the crowd in Pilate's hall' in *Hymns of Faith and Hope* (London: James Nesbitt, 1857) 207-208.

Father's will. Their error was to infer that God must crown every effort of a true Messiah with success and that Jesus' agony was proof of the falsity of his pretensions – not knowing that God would vindicate his Son at the resurrection.

The Sufferer of Psalm 69:20

Movement 29, a tenor *accompagnato*, is a setting of Psalm 69:20.[12]

David, the writer of the psalm, is faced with persecution and expresses his deep distress. As with many of the psalms written by David (who, in a sense, was God's anointed one or a 'Christ'), this psalm consists not only of personal reflections but has a wider horizon – it is a song of the Christ, the Messiah. For example, verse 9 of the psalm ('For zeal for your house has consumed me') is quoted in John 2:17 as applying to Jesus' action of cleansing the Temple. Jesus himself states in John 15:25 that part of verse 4 of the psalm ('those who hate me without cause') is to be fulfilled in the imminent cross of Calvary. The apostle John would appear to have verse 21 of the psalm in mind, when he records how Jesus was given sour wine to drink (John 19:29).

Some may question whether verses 22–28 of the psalm, with David pronouncing curses on his tormentors, are in line with the spirit of Jesus who prayed for those tormenting him (Luke 23:34). But such verses – as indeed similar sections in other so-called 'Imprecatory Psalms' – remind us of the reality of judgement (as was discussed earlier in connection with Part I, Scenes 2 and 5). Jesus himself pronounced 'woes' on the scribes and Pharisees (Matt 23:13–36). He spoke of himself saying to some on the day 'when the Son of Man comes in his glory' (Matt 25:31), 'Depart from me, you cursed, into the eternal fire prepared for the devil and his angels' (Matt 25:41). Today, however, we still live in 'the day of salvation' (2 Cor 6:2). On the cross Jesus prayed for forgiveness for those who nailed him there (Luke 23:34) and he assured the penitent thief of a place in Paradise with him that very day (Luke 23:43). Grace and mercy are still freely

[12] As elsewhere, the first person of the Bible text is changed to the third person. In the *Book of Common Prayer* Psalter, from which this verse is taken, the verse number is 21 (not 20), as a result of verse 13 of the Psalm, as it appears in most Bible versions, being made into two separate verses in the *Book of Common Prayer* – with a knock-on effect on all subsequent verses in this psalm.

available for all who ask for it: the day which will bring with it the awful reality of judgement for those who are unprepared has not yet dawned.

So, with the full encouragement of the approach of the New Testament towards Palm 69, we should have no hesitation in regarding statements within this psalm as windows through which to view the Lord Jesus Christ where such connections are appropriate.

Verse 20 (the verse used at this point in the oratorio) can rightly be taken in such a way. In this verse David laments: 'Reproaches have broken my heart, so that I am in despair.' A more intensely desperate sense of personal suffering within the very core of an individual's being can hardly be imagined. The *Book of Common Prayer* rendering used here, *'Thy reproach'*, which attributes the action to God is, sadly, inaccurate, even though it neatly fits into the flow of the argument in this scene of *Messiah* and is very suggestive of Christ's cry of dereliction on the cross.

A better approach to verse 20 is to begin with the previous verse of the psalm, where David speaks of his 'reproach' and 'shame' and 'dishonour' (Ps 69:19). Such terms are highly fitting in connection with crucifixion, a criminal's death, and Hebrews 12:2 specifically mentions 'the shame' of the cross that Jesus endured. Psalm 69:20 enters into the sense of forsakenness that Jesus experienced on the cross – here not so much being forsaken by the Father, although we know that this was supremely what his spiritual agony consisted of – but rather being forsaken by anyone who might have offered some crumb of human comfort. In the Garden of Gethsemane, just before the arrest, Jesus asked Peter, James and John to sit with him and to watch while he prayed, but three times they fell asleep and left him to his agony alone (Matt 26:36–46). We know that the apostle John was present at the foot of the cross and so too was his mother and a few women in Jesus' company, including Mary Magdalene (John 19:25–27, Matt 27:55–56, Luke 23:49). It is possible that Peter also was there, for he describes himself in his first letter as 'a witness of the sufferings of Christ' (1 Pet 5:1). But none of them was able to provide Jesus with the understanding and sympathy which he desired. *'Comfort'* is promised to God's people (Isa 40:1, Movement 2) but it is denied to the Messiah as he is crucified.

The Sufferer of Lamentations 1:12

Movement 30 is an *arioso* (or short air) sung by the tenor and is a setting of the central part of Lamentations 1:12: Lamentations was written in about 575 BC, probably by Jeremiah, and it consists of a series of meditations on the fall of Jerusalem at the hands of the Babylonian invaders. It has to be admitted that this Bible book is sorely neglected today, except for the well-known verses, Lamentations 3:22–23:

> The steadfast love of the Lord never ceases;
> his mercies never come to an end;
> they are new every morning;
> great is your faithfulness.

These are very nearly the central words of this well-crafted book. But they stand out as statements of the Lord's 'steadfast love' and 'mercies' and 'faithfulness' all the more strikingly because they are surrounded by five chapters which speak of the bitter suffering of God's people, in particular the plight of Jerusalem: 'How like a widow she has become, she who was great among the nations!' (Lam 1:1).

It is possible that Jennens turned to Lamentations 1:12 because of its reference to *'sorrow'*, thereby following up the specific references to *'sorrows'* in Isaiah 53:3–4 (Movements 23 and 24). The words of Lamentations 1:12 are in the first person in the Bible text, once again transferred to the third person in Jennens's libretto. They are words spoken by Jerusalem about her *'sorrow'*, which she claims is far more bitter than any other sorrow that could be uncovered anywhere.

The question has to be asked: Is Jennens right to put the words of Lamentations 1:12 on the lips of the Messiah hanging on the cross? The answer has to be both 'no' and 'yes':

First, 'no' – because they are words spoken by sinful Jerusalem, who is deeply aware that her sorrow is a punishment from God ('which the Lord inflicted on the day of his fierce anger', v 12c). Jerusalem, we are told in verse 8, 'sinned grievously.' She is described as 'filthy' (v 8) and her 'uncleanness' (v 9) is obvious to all – and these words refer to her immorality with her 'lovers' (v 2): what is meant is Judah's spiritual immorality in abandoning the worship of Yahweh for that of other deities, but the worship of those other deities (Baal and Asherah) involved physical immorality too. She admits, 'The Lord is in the right, for I have rebelled against his word' (v 18).

But, secondly, 'yes' – because the Messiah has identified himself so clearly with his people's needs, even to the extent of taking their 'infirmities' and their sins upon himself. We have seen this most clearly in the earlier discussion of the suffering servant of Isaiah 53, who has *'borne our griefs and carried our sorrows',* (Isa 53:4). *'The Lord hath laid on him the iniquity of us all'* (Isa 53:6) and he has taken our punishment in our place. God did bring unimaginable *'sorrow'* on his beloved Son: to use again the wording of Lamentations 1:12, he 'inflicted' it on the first Good Friday, which was 'the day of his fierce anger' – far fiercer than God's anger on the day when he brought about the destruction of Jerusalem by the Babylonians. In fact, traditionally this text has become frequently associated with Good Friday. So, although it may not be what the writer of Lamentations had in mind as the primary reference, Lamentations 1:12 can be rightly understood as an expression of the sufferings of Christ on behalf of his people.

As we come to the end of Scene 1 of Part II, this long and important section focusing on the substitutionary work of the Lord Jesus Christ, we should pause and consider the question and appeal with which Lamentations 1:12 begins: 'Is it nothing to you, all you who pass by? Look and see'. In John Stainer's oratorio *The Crucifixion* (the text selected by John William Sparrow-Simpson) the whole of this verse is sung as a bass recitative immediately before a chorus entitled 'The Appeal of the Crucified' with the following words:

> From the Throne of His Cross, the King of grief
> cries out to a world of unbelief:
> Oh! men and women, afar and nigh,
> is it nothing to you, all ye that pass by?
> I laid my eternal power aside,
> I came from the home of the glorified,
> a babe, in the lowly cave to lie;
> is it nothing to you, all ye that pass by?
> I wept for the sorrows and pains of men,
> I healed them, and helped them, and loved
> them; but then
> they shouted against me, Crucify!

Is it nothing to you, all ye that pass by?
Behold me and see: pierced through and through
with countless sorrows and all is for you;
for you I suffer, for you I die;
is it nothing to you, all ye that pass by?
Oh! men and women, your deeds of shame,
your sins without reason and number and
name,
I bear them all on this Cross on high;
is it nothing to you, all ye that pass by?
Is it nothing to you that I bow my head?
And nothing to you that my blood is shed?
Oh perishing souls, to you I cry;
is it nothing to you, all ye that pass by?
Oh come unto me! by the woes I have borne,
by the dreadful scourge, and the crown of
thorn,
by these I implore you to hear my cry;
is it nothing to you, all ye that pass by?
Oh come unto me! This awful price,
redemption's tremendous sacrifice,
is paid for you. Oh, why will ye die?
Is it nothing to you, all ye that pass by?[13]

The apostle Paul could never get over his wonder and amazement at the grace of a Saviour–God who reached down to rescue such a needy sinner as he knew himself to be. He writes of living 'by faith in the Son of God, who loved *me* and gave himself for *me*' (my italics, Gal 2:20).

[13] John Stainer, *The Crucifixion*, 1887.

What to listen out for in the music in Part II Scene 1

There is a marked change of tone in the music in this scene, which is totally appropriate for its subject matter. Many, but not all, of the movements are set in the minor key and Handel produces powerful effects of dramatic intensity.

In this scene, we notice a difference in the role of choruses. In contrast to the choruses of Part I, which all breathed an atmosphere of brightness and uplift, the choruses in this first scene of Part II are more reflective and, for the most part, solemn in their mood.

There is a change in the function of choruses throughout Part II. In Part I all the choruses except one marked the conclusion of a scene – the exception being the additional chorus at the end of Movement 9, halfway through Scene 3. Used in this way the Part I, choruses round off each scene with a note of emphasis. By contrast, the choruses in Part II are more integral to the unfolding of the drama. They are used more frequently in Part II, with 11 of the 23 movements being choruses, as opposed to choruses making up just 5½ of the 21 movements of Part I.

22. Chorus: *'Behold the Lamb of God'*

This opening item of Part II is a striking example of Handel's skill in producing items of dramatic intensity. The chorus begins like a French overture in a minor key, which – as we have noticed before – so often suggests a mood of mournfulness.

The slow tempo of the piece (it is marked as *largo*) serves to draw out the deeply significant words of the text, pointing to Jesus as the one who would die for the sins of the world.

The contrapuntal style of the voices' opening bars, repeatedly reinforcing the words of the text, adds significantly to the impact.

At the beginning, the *continuo* drops an octave, then the violins rise an octave to express the phrase which the voices will sing for *'Behold the Lamb of God'*. The contraltos begin, followed at half-bar intervals by the sopranos, the basses and finally the tenors. After the initial octave leap, the melody falls in dotted rhythms, but rises on *'that taketh away the sin of the world'*.

The melody shows similarity to the beginning of Movement 20, *'He shall feed his flock'*, but here it is made more poignant partly by being in a minor key (rather than major) and also by the use of dotted rhythm (rather than the smoother triplets of Movement 20).

23. Air: *'He was despised and rejected of men'*

This air is the longest movement in the oratorio in terms of duration and conveys the Messiah's *'despised and rejected'* condition with great poignancy.

It is a *da capo* air, (otherwise known as an air in ternary form), which means that it has an A-B-A structure, with A representing the musical setting of Isaiah 53:3a and B representing the middle section, the setting of Isaiah 50:6. As such, the air expresses two contrasting moods, emphasised by the two different keys: Eb major for the outside sections and the related key of C minor for the middle section.

The vocal line begins with another occurrence of the now familiar ascending fourth on *'He was'* and adds another one on *'despised'*. A further one is used on *'a man'* (at the start of the phrase *'a man of sorrows'*).

Handel breaks the beginning of the text into a stammering *'he was despised – despised and rejected – a man of sorrows'*. All this is so suggestive of Christ's agony. A little later, the phrases *'He was despised'* and *'rejected'* are interspersed with rests as long as the words, as if exhausted. Soft, sighing motifs from the violins, an echo of the singing, drop into these rests. A little later the words *'he was despised'* and *'rejected'* are sung unaccompanied, and this feature can be regarded as suggestive of Christ's abandonment.

The contrasting middle section is full of dramatic rests for the soloist, but now the voice is set against a ceaseless agitated pattern of fast dotted notes from the instruments, illustrating the beating of *'the smiters'* referred to in the text.

24. Chorus: *'Surely he hath borne our griefs and carried our sorrows'*

It is worth noting the fact that at this point Handel provides three consecutive chorus items in Movements 24, 25 and 26. This is particularly fitting for the settings of a sequence of verses from Isaiah 53, which – as was commented on above – are intensely personal in a collective way.

This chorus, as I suggested earlier, is possibly the most moving of all in the oratorio. Not surprisingly, it is set in a minor key – F minor.

For much of the movement, the orchestral accompaniment consists of dotted rhythms, as in the middle part of the previous movement, creating an agitated effect, suggestive either of the servant's suffering or of the believers' anguished response of awe – or of both.

The twice-repeated *'surely'*, at the beginning of the chorus, further intensifies the atmosphere, as the onlookers take to heart the unexpected truth being expressed here.

25. Chorus: *'And with his stripes we are healed'*

This chorus continues in the same minor key but its mood is in complete contrast. A more joyful tone pervades the piece, reflecting a mood of beneficial release for those who previously were suffering from their spiritual infirmities.

The chorus represents a good example of contrapuntal writing. The theme begins with a sequence of long notes, which Mozart quoted in the 'Kyrie' fugue of his 'Requiem.'

The characteristic ascending fourth opens the countersubject (on the words *'and with'*), introducing the phrase *'and with his stripes we are healed.'*

The word *'healed'* is later stressed by both long *melismas* and long notes (as explained earlier on, a *melisma* means one syllable flowering out into a passage of several notes).

26. Chorus: *'All we like sheep have gone astray'*

In this chorus, the key of F minor gives way to F major, thus giving most of this movement (except for the last 17 bars) an atmosphere of joy, even playfulness. Handel makes use of musical onomatopoeia in this movement. The voices utter twice together, *'All we like sheep.'* Then two voice parts (sopranos and tenors) move simultaneously in different directions on *'have gone astray'*, with the last syllable extended to eleven notes. The next part of the text, *'we have turned'*, is illustrated by fast *coloraturas*, lacking direction. All this is so suggestive of a flock of wandering sheep.

The thoughtful listener's first reaction may be one of surprise at the tone of this chorus which appears out of place – even frivolous – when the subject matter is so serious. But surely Handel's intention is that the light-hearted mood is an expression of the former carefree abandon of foolish *'sheep'* who used to take perverse delight in the fact that they *'have gone astray'*. In the context of the Servant Song, the onlookers now penitently admit their past folly, but the musical setting captures the mood of their earlier spiritual carelessness. So it is only appropriate that the music should express the mindless meandering of lost sheep – the way this group of onlookers (the *'we'* of Isaiah 53) once were.

Handel's setting of the first part of verse 6 runs to several pages of the musical score, which is a skilful move, because it throws into sharp relief his setting, in the last 17 bars, of the second half of the verse, where the mood becomes totally different. In a dramatic sudden *adagio*, full of chromatic tension, the movement ends on the powerful words, *'and the Lord hath laid on him the iniquity of us all.'* The contrapuntal introduction to this closing *adagio* section intensifies the announcement that it is God who takes the initiative in atonement, as we hear from each of the four voices in turn the three words *'and the Lord'* before we hear the continuation of this phrase: *'hath laid on him the iniquity of us all'*. The striking harmonies, effectively returning the key to F minor, powerfully engage the listener's attention.

27. *Accompagnato: 'All they that see him laugh him to scorn'*

Dotted rhythm in the accompaniment to this item creates an atmosphere of agitated tension.

The strings play violent figures after *'laugh him to scorn'* and *'shoot out their lips'*, similar to an outburst of laughter.

28. Chorus: *'He trusted in God that he would deliver him'*

This substantial chorus is a strict fugue in C minor – until the closing few bars in block chord style.

The chorus acts as the crowd of onlookers (senior clerics and ordinary passers-by) separately hurling their insults at the one who suffers on the cross.

29. *Accompagnato: 'Thy rebuke hath broken his heart'*

This item is extremely poignant. Aching chromatic chords picture the broken heart. The *accompagnato* begins in one key (Ab major), but it shifts without stability and ends in a totally different key (B major). This has to be understood as a musical expression of anguish.

30. Arioso: *'Behold, and see if there be any sorrow like unto his sorrow!'*

An *arioso*, as the word suggests, is a type of air (or aria) but it tends to be a short, sustained, developed and dignified vocal piece, as is true of this item.

A striking feature of this short movement in E minor is the way the accompaniment pauses rather regularly on the first and third beat of the bar. The effect of this device is to give all the more weight to the soloist's words.

Part II Scene 2: The Messiah's Death and Resurrection

31. ***Accompagnato*** **(tenor)**
He was cut off out of the land of the living; for the transgression of thy people was he stricken. (Isaiah 53:8)

32. Air (tenor)
But thou didst not leave his soul in hell; nor didst thou suffer thy Holy One to see corruption. (Psalm 16:10)

The Messiah's death: Isaiah 53:8

It may come as a surprise that the Messiah's death is dealt with in only one movement (Movement 31), a tenor *accompagnato* consisting of only five bars. But the previous scene, the most substantial of all in the work, has dealt with the redemptive sufferings of the Lord Jesus Christ (or his 'passion', to use the technical term, which derives from the Latin word 'to suffer'). It is what Jesus endured for our sakes while on the cross that achieved our salvation. So all that needs to be recorded at this point in Handel's oratorio is the fact that Jesus' suffering on behalf of fallen humanity came to an end when he actually died, or 'breathed his last' (Mark 15:37), or 'gave up his spirit' (John 19:30).

When we talk about what Jesus accomplished for us on the cross, the New Testament normally refers simply to his death, for example when Paul, writing to the Corinthians, states that 'Christ died for our sins according to the Scriptures' (1 Cor 15:3). But really such statements are a shorthand way of referring to the sum total of his 'passion', in other words, his redemptive sufferings on the cross – what is sometimes spoken of as his 'cross work'.

At this point, in Movement 31, the text is Isaiah 53:8, which – like the earlier verses from this Bible chapter in the previous scene – focuses on the Suffering Servant. *'Cut off'* is a violent verb: a synonym might be 'hacked off'. The fact that the servant is *'cut off out of the land of the living'* leaves no doubt that Jesus 'was crucified, died and was buried', to quote from the Apostles' Creed. And we are reminded once more that Jesus' death was an act of substitutionary atonement: *'for the transgression of thy people was he stricken.'*

The Messiah's resurrection: Psalm 16:10

If the oratorio's treatment of Jesus' actual death seems at first sight surprisingly brief, the same can be said about the treatment of Jesus' resurrection, covered by the tenor air of Movement 32. The note of victory is not yet fully reflected at this stage in Handel's *Messiah.* In fact, the tone at this point is somewhat subdued. This is a moment for solemn reflection. Triumphant celebration will follow in later movements. Part III of the oratorio deals particularly with the resurrection of Jesus Christ and the future resurrection of Christian believers. For now, we are invited simply to take in the truth that 'on the third day he rose again', to quote again from the Apostles' Creed.

The text of Movement 32 is taken from Psalm 16:10. The psalm is written by David and in it he expresses the confidence (for both this life and beyond) that comes from having a personal relationship with God, the one in whom he takes refuge (v 1). In verses 9–11, he speaks of his present joy in knowing that death will not be the end, 'For you will not abandon my soul to Sheol, or let your holy one see corruption' (v 10).

The two parts of this verse are parallelisms: David identifies himself as God's 'holy one' (or 'faithful one', in the NIV footnote).

Although this is a personal statement by David concerning his own future security beyond death, both Peter and Paul, in speeches in Acts, argue that Psalm 16 is a messianic psalm. Therefore, properly understood at a deeper level, it refers not to David but to the Messiah, Jesus.

Peter, in his Pentecost sermon on behalf of himself and his fellow apostles, quotes verses 8–11 of the psalm in the Septuagint version in Acts 2:25–28, and adds the comment:

> Brothers, I may say to you with confidence about the patriarch David that he both died and was buried, and his tomb is with us to this day. Being therefore a prophet, and knowing that God had sworn with an oath that he would set one of his descendants on his

> throne, he foresaw and spoke about the resurrection of the Christ, that he was not abandoned to Hades, nor did his flesh see corruption. This Jesus God raised up, and of that we all are witnesses (Acts 2:29–32).

The promise of God to David about a king to come from his line is the messianic promise of 2 Samuel 7:12–14.

Paul makes essentially the same point in his quotation of Psalm 16:10 in his sermon at Pisidian Antioch in Acts 13:35–37. David, he says, died and was buried, and his body decayed. 'But he whom God raised up [in other words, Jesus] did not see corruption' (Acts 13:37).

As we have come to expect in Jennens's quotations from Psalms, he uses the *Book of Common Prayer* version.[1] However, he deliberately changes the two future tenses of the verse into past tenses, in order to underline the New Testament understanding that, for those who live in the post-resurrection era, this verse speaks no longer of a future prophecy but of a past historical event.

The resurrection of Jesus enables us to view the cross in the right way. On Good Friday, Jesus was condemned; on Easter Day, he was vindicated. If the message at first appeared to be a tragic one (Jesus defeated), the full message of that weekend is now revealed as: Jesus defeated sin and death and hell. The victory won on the cross is followed by the victory parade of the resurrection. The Son's 'It is finished!' is answered by the Father's 'Amen!' Jesus' rising again is evidence that the sacrifice of Calvary was indeed effective. The wrath of God is satisfied and the price is paid for mankind's sin.

In an earlier age, when a person owed money and could not pay, he was put in a debtors' prison until he could pay his debts. But if a debtor went into hiding, someone who had given assurances of that person's character might be put into the debtors' prison instead. So, if A was in debt and went into hiding, B (his guarantor) would be imprisoned in his place. But if A, from his hiding place, subsequently saw B walking along the road free, he would know that his debt had been paid and that there was no

---

[1] In the Psalter of the *Book of Common Prayer* the text appears as verse 11, not verse 10.

further danger to face from the law. In the same way, the man or woman who trusts in Christ can be assured from the fact of Jesus' physical resurrection that their debt towards God has been cleared – the slate is wiped clean.

There is an inevitability about Jesus' resurrection. Again quoting Peter in his Pentecost sermon, 'God raised him up, loosing the pangs of death, because *it was not possible* for him to be held by it' (Acts 2:24, my italics).

The reference in the comments on the previous scene to the death of Aslan in C S Lewis's *The Lion, the Witch and the Wardrobe* was accompanied by the promise of a follow-up comment on the sequel to that episode. Aslan comes to life again and explains how the Witch did not know 'that when a willing victim who had committed no treachery was killed in a traitor's stead, the Table would crack and Death itself would start working backwards.'[2] 'Death ... working backwards' is a powerful pictorial definition of resurrection.

'He descended into hell'

Did Jesus go to hell between his death and resurrection? The wording of Psalm 16:10 in the AV (and in the version of Psalms in the *Book of Common Prayer* used in the text of the oratorio) might lead us to this understanding. So too might the wording of the Apostles' Creed in the *Book of Common Prayer*: 'And he descended into hell.' Also Jennens's original title for this scene might suggest the same: 'His sacrificial death, His passage through Hell and resurrection.' But, in fact, these usages of the word 'hell' reflect a different meaning of the word from that in modern-day English. Nevertheless, as we shall discover, Jesus did experience hell, in the truest sense of the word, but this happened before he died, and not afterwards.

In the AV, the word 'hell' in the Old Testament translates the Hebrew word 'Sheol'. It would be less confusing to follow the ESV, rather than the NIV, and use the word 'Sheol' rather than 'hell'. Sheol signifies the place of the departed and it covers the situation beyond death of both righteous, godly believers and also the wicked. But David was clear in his understanding that Sheol was not the final and everlasting destiny of the godly believer. That is the confidence he expresses in the closing verses

[2] Lewis, *The Lion, the Witch and the Wardrobe*, 148.

of Psalm 16, the psalm of Movement 32, in as far as these verses apply to himself, without exploring the deeper layer of messianic prophecy. The final verse of Psalm 16 expresses David's certainty about his future, as typical of all faithful Israelites: 'You make known to me the path of life; in your presence there is fullness of joy; at your right hand are pleasures for evermore' (Ps 16:11).

When we come into the New Testament, we find two words that are translated as 'hell'. As with 'Sheol', it is probably most helpful to retain the original words in their Anglicised forms.

One of these two words is 'Hades', which represents the world of death and is the equivalent of Old Testament 'Sheol.' The rich man in Jesus' parable of Luke 16 was in Hades (Luke 16:23), and so too was Jesus immediately following his death (Acts 2:27, quoting Psalm 16:10, as we have already seen). Jesus' descent into Hades and his defeat of death transform death and Hades for the Christian believer. That is why the ascended and glorified Christ says of himself, 'I died, and behold, I am alive for evermore, and I have the keys of Death and Hades' (Rev 1:18). It is in the light of the resurrection that we can understand Jesus' promise that 'the gates of Hades shall not prevail against' his church (Matt 16:18). What a tremendous assurance from Jesus himself that the church can never die! Nowhere in the New Testament is there any hint that, in the time from Jesus' resurrection onwards, any Christian who dies goes to Hades. Rather, for Christian believers there is the assurance that they go to be with Christ, which is far better (Phil 1:23), and that being with Christ in Paradise, or heaven, is the Christian believer's experience from the moment of death, as was promised to the penitent criminal crucified with Jesus ('today' – Luke 23:43).

The other New Testament word, which represents the place of eternal punishment, is 'Gehenna' – a name that derives from the Greek form of the Valley of Hinnom in Jerusalem, where children were sacrificed by fire in connection with pagan rites (2 Kings 23:10) and where, later, the city's rubbish was thrown and constantly burnt. What comes as a surprise to many people is the fact that, apart from one reference to Gehenna in the Letter of James (James 3:8), all other instances of the word are to be found on the lips of Jesus (for example, Matt 5:29–30).

We need to be aware also that this understanding of 'hell' is conveyed not only by the word 'Gehenna', but also by other equivalent expressions. For example, what is implied by the word 'perish' as the stark alternative to 'have eternal life' in the well-known John 3:16, with the implication that this destiny too is of an 'eternal' nature; or the fiery furnace into which all causes of sin and all law-breakers will be thrown (Matt 13:43, 25:41); or 'the punishment of eternal destruction, away from the presence of the Lord and from the glory of his might' (2 Thess 1:9). This understanding of separation from God is the essence of 'hell' (in other words, Gehenna).

It is not popular today to preach on hell (in other words, Gehenna) – as we noted in connection with Movements 5–7, the reality of a future judgement is largely dismissed in modern society. Sir Arthur Conan Doyle spoke for many when he wrote, 'Hell, I may say ... has long dropped out of the thoughts of every reasonable man.'[3] Michael Paternoster commented a few decades ago, 'Hell is a real embarrassment to the modern Christian, who prefers not to think about it, and a real stumbling-block to the non-Christian, who rightly insists on thinking about it.'[4]

Paul's exposition of the gospel in his letter to the Romans leaves no doubt that 'the wrath of God' is both the *present* divine response towards 'all ungodliness and unrighteousness of men' (Rom 1:18) and the *future* destiny of all who do not trust in Christ in order to be 'saved by him' (Rom 5:9). This perspective on gospel-proclamation, as being the means of a real rescue from the prospect of hell (in other words, Gehenna), has been the motivation of the evangelistic work of Christian preachers and missionaries down the centuries. The words of two Christian leaders will serve to illustrate this concern. First, John Wesley, in a letter in March 1748, wrote:

> In plain terms, whenever I see one or a thousand men running into Hell, be it in England, Ireland, or France, yea, in Europe, Asia, Africa, or America, I will stop them if I can; as a minister of Christ, I will beseech them in His name to turn back and be reconciled to God. Were I to try to do otherwise, were I to let any soul drop into the pit whom I might have saved from everlasting burnings, I am not satisfied that God

---

[3] Cited in H. Buis, *The Doctrine of Eternal Punishment* (Grand Rapids: Baker Book House, 1957), 146.

[4] M. Paternoster, *Thou Art There Also* (London: SPCK, 1967), 14.

> would accept my pleas, 'Lord, he was not of my parish.'[5]

Second, Hudson Taylor, the pioneer missionary to China said, 'I would never have thought of going out to China, had I not believed that the Chinese were lost and needed Christ'.[6] The force of that word 'lost' needs to be given due consideration. At the age of 18, he had written to his younger sister:

> I have a stronger desire than ever to go to China. That land is ever in my thoughts. Think of it – 360 million souls, without God or hope in the world! ... dying ... without any of the consolations of the Gospel.[7]

Christian preachers must be faithful in their teaching about the 'last things' (death, judgement, heaven and hell), but in so doing there should be no relish or triumphalism in spelling out the terrible consequences that inevitably result from refusing to believe in Jesus. He is the one who alone has 'the words of eternal life' (John 6.:68) and who, as we have seen earlier, pleads with people, 'Come to me ... and I will give you rest' (Matt.11:28). D L Moody spoke profoundly when he said, 'When we preach hell, we might at least do it with tears in our eyes.'[8] And this is simply to follow the example of Jesus himself. Luke records two incidents when Jesus grieves over Jerusalem and the judgement that would fall on it at the hands of the Romans within a generation. On the one occasion he says, 'O Jerusalem, Jerusalem, the city that kills the prophets and stones those who are sent to it! How often would I have gathered your children together as a hen gathers her brood under his wings, and you would not!' (Luke 13:34). On the other occasion when Jesus speaks similar words, we are told that 'when he drew near and saw the city, he wept over it' (Luke 19:41).

---

[5] Cited in Dick Dowsett, *God, That's Not Fair!* (Bromley: STL Books, 1982), 49.
[6] Dowsett, *God That's Not Fair!,* 55.
[7] Doswett, *God That's Not Fair!,* 55.
[8] Cited in S. Gregg, *All You Want to Know about Hell: Three Christian Views of God's Final Solution to the Problem of Sin* (Nashville: Thomas Nelson, 2013), 299.

So what was the experience of Jesus? In what sense did he 'go to hell'? From all that has been discussed in the comments in the previous scene of *Messiah,* and in this scene too, it will be clear that Jesus endured the bitterest pains of hell (in other words, Gehenna) while he suffered on the cross. He experienced separation from the Father, if not for an eternity of time, certainly to an eternity of degree (if we may use the word 'eternity' in that way). Jesus suffered hell so that all those who come to him in repentance and faith will be delivered from the terrors of hell. But when Jesus died, he had completed the work of salvation – 'It is finished' (John 19:30). ''Tis done – the great transaction's done', as Philip Doddridge's hymn 'O Happy Day' puts it.[9] After the cross, Jesus did not go to hell (in other words, Gehenna) for he had already overcome it – but, to quote again from the older version of the Apostles' Creed, he 'descended into hell' in the sense of 'Hades', because he truly died.

What to listen out for in the music in Part II Scene 2

31. *Accompagnato: 'He was cut off out of the land of the living'*

After all the drama of the previous scene, this short *accompagnato* announces the fact of the Messiah's death in a restrained way.

32. Air: *'But thou didst not leave his soul in hell'*

There is a restrained tone to this air too, despite its announcement of the Messiah's resurrection, allowing later movements to revel in the joy of this great truth.

[9] Philip Doddridge, 'O Happy Day', in *Hymns, Founded on Various Texts in the Holy Scriptures* (1755).

Part II Scene 3: The Messiah's Ascension

33. Chorus

Lift up your heads, O ye gates, and be ye lift up, ye everlasting doors, and the King of glory shall come in. Who is this King of glory? The Lord strong and mighty, the Lord mighty in battle.

Lift up your heads, O ye gates, and be ye lift up, ye everlasting doors, and the King of glory shall come in! Who is this King of glory? The Lord of hosts, he is the King of glory. (Psalm 24:7–10)

The King of glory: Psalm 24:7–10

This scene is made up of only one movement, Movement 33, which is a chorus consisting of four verses from the end of Psalm 24. Psalm 24 is traditionally used on Ascension Day, so we should not be surprised at Jennens's selection of this text for a scene focusing on Christ's ascension. No doubt he was drawn to it, as he clearly took so much delight in illustrating New Testament truth from the Old Testament.

In the flow of the oratorio, this chorus plays a significant role. After the strong emphasis in the first ten movements of Part II on the sufferings of the Messiah, and a somewhat restrained statement of his resurrection in the preceding movement, we are now given a triumphant announcement that he has indeed won the victory through all that he endured. He is in truth *'the King of glory ... the Lord strong and mighty ... the Lord mighty in battle ... the Lord of hosts.'* The verses from Psalm 24 helpfully establish a link between Jesus' ascension and his kingship. Indeed, the Ascension might well be described as Jesus' coronation – his exaltation to 'the highest place' and his sitting down 'at the right hand of the Majesty in heaven', to pick up phrases from Philippians 2:10 and Hebrews 1:3.

Apart from such New Testament verses as these last two which refer to the truth of Christ's ascension, it is only in the two volumes of Luke that we are given an account of the Ascension itself: a brief account at the very end of his Gospel (Luke 24:50–53) and an expanded account at the beginning of Acts (1:1–11). In addition, Jesus refers to his coming ascension in his words to Mary Magdalene in John 20:17. In the whole of the Bible, it is only in Acts 1:3 where the date of the Ascension is stated – namely 40 days after the resurrection, and therefore ten days before Pentecost.

Jesus' ascension had to happen. The post-resurrection appearances, important as they were in establishing the truth of Jesus' bodily rising again (see, for example, 1 Cor 15:3–8), could not continue indefinitely. Christian converts would have flocked to Judea in an attempt to see the risen Christ for themselves in ever-increasing numbers. But it would have been impossible for the Christian church over the centuries to have enjoyed the presence of Christ on the sporadic basis of those post-Easter appearances. During his earthly ministry, Jesus could only be in one place at any one time, and that includes the post-Easter appearances. Still today, physically in his glorified person, he is in the single location of the throne of heaven. But since the Day of Pentecost, when the Holy Spirit came to take Jesus' place according to his promise (for example, John 14:16–17), Jesus has been – and continues to be – with all Christians in all places at all times by his Spirit.

Martin Luther included these words in an Ascension sermon:

> We must think of his lordship and his ascension as something active, ongoing, working, and must not let ourselves think that he is sitting up above, remote and isolated, while we are managing everything down here below. No! He ascended up thither for the simple reason that it is there that he can perform properly his real work, and from there exercise his lordship. Had he remained on earth in visible form before the people, he could not have wrought so effectually, for all the people could not have been with him and heard him all the time.
>
> For this reason he inaugurated his ascension as an expediency which makes it possible for him to be in touch with all and to reign in all at one and the same time; to preach to all, and be heard by all, and to abide

> with all. Therefore, beware of imagining that he has gone, and is now remote and far from us. The opposite is true. It was while he was on earth that he was far from us; now he is most near.[1]

Psalm 24 begins with an affirmation of the Lord's ownership of the world that he has made and its people (v 1–2). It then poses a question: by what right do we come into the Lord's presence (v 3)? And the answer has to be: by holiness of our whole being (v 4). The problem is, of course, that we are in no way, by ourselves, holy people. The Bible's testimony to this depressing reality has been set out clearly in the earlier movements of Part II of *Messiah.* But Psalm 24 also tells us that those who 'seek' the Lord (the word is used twice in verse 6) will receive 'righteousness from God' (v 5). For such an individual, the Lord is 'the God of his salvation' (v 5). Here is an anticipation of Paul's teaching that 'justification' (or 'righteousness', the same word in the Greek) is a gift of God to be received by faith (Rom 3:24; Eph 2:8). Implicit too in Psalm 24 is the reality that the worshipper who intends to 'ascend the hill of the Lord' and 'stand in his holy place' (in other words, come to the Jerusalem temple) will present the appropriate offering to be sacrificed on the altar, which was the prescribed way in Old Testament times to deal with sin. And that continued to be the appropriate way to approach God until Jesus came and died on the cross as the once-for-all sacrifice to end all sacrifices (Heb 10:10–14).

The closing verses of Psalm 24, which we find in this movement of the oratorio, pose a second question: by what right does the Lord come among us (v 7–10)? The answer is that he is *'the King of glory', 'the Lord of hosts.'* He is the Sovereign, as the opening two verses of the psalm announced – and, in the light of verses 3–6, his sovereignty includes the realm of redemption. *'Lift up your heads, O ye gates, and be ye lift up, ye everlasting doors'* could be paraphrased as 'Fling wide the gates: open the ancient doors.' In ancient culture, doors were often taken off their hinges when people wanted to show their welcome to a distinguished guest. Some doors were drawn up and down like a portcullis and may have protruded from the top, literally lifting their heads. So we are given a

---

[1] Cited in J. Atkinson (ed.), *The Darkness of Faith: Daily Readings with Martin Luther* (London: Darton, Longman and Todd, 1987), 57.

picture of heaven's gate being opened wide as the Lord enters, fresh from his victory in securing salvation.

What to listen out for in the music in Part II Scene 3

33. Chorus: *'Lift up your heads'*

This chorus presents some interesting features. Handel takes full advantage of the two-person conversation suggested by the text of Psalm 24:7–10. So he divides the voices into two groups.

The first group, consisting of sopranos (separated into first and second sopranos) and contraltos, sings verse 7, summoning the gates to be opened for the King of glory's entry. The second group, consisting of tenors and basses, sings the question of verse 8a, *'Who is this King of glory?'* and is answered by the first group with the words of verse 8b.

For verses 9 and 10 (which are essentially a repeat of verses 7 and 8), the roles are reversed for the first part of the 'conversation' with the tenors and basses (plus the contraltos, now singing in both groups, in order to provide three-part harmony) opening the exchange.

But Handel quickly moves into all four voices (the sopranos now singing as one part) to make the most of the triumphant answer to the question of the King's identity. This full-blooded celebration makes up over half of the movement.

Part II Scene 4: The Messiah's Exaltation

34. Recitative (tenor)
Unto which of the angels said he at any time, Thou art my Son, this day have I begotten thee? (Hebrews 1:5a)

35. Chorus
Let all the angels of God worship him. (Hebrews 1:6b)

The Son whom angels worship (Hebrews 1)

To all intents and purposes, this short scene can be regarded as an extension of the previous one. Jennens, however, intended it as a separate scene with the title 'God discloses His identity in heaven.' He makes use of a couple of half-verses from Hebrews 1: verses 5a and 6b.

The purpose of the Letter to the Hebrews was to encourage Jewish Christians to continue in their faith in Jesus Christ, despite huge pressures put on them – culturally, religiously, emotionally, economically, even physically – to give up their Christian profession and return to their former Judaism. The exhortation to 'hold fast' to their 'confidence' (for example, Heb 3:6) is repeated frequently. One of the great themes of the letter is the superiority of Christ, in every respect, to anything that Judaism had to offer. Indeed, his coming has fulfilled great Old Testament themes, not least sacrifice and priesthood, and in so doing he has rendered temple-sacrifices and the Levitical priesthood obsolete. To return to these Old Testament practices and rituals would, in effect, be to revert to the 'shadow of the good things to come instead of the true form of these realities' (Heb 10:1).

Hebrews 1, after an important introductory paragraph concerning the final word that God has spoken through his Son and the finished work accomplished by Christ, concerns the superiority of Jesus as God's Son to the angels. In order to prove his point, the writer of this letter appeals to texts from the Old Testament. Those harassing the Jewish Christians would have regarded such texts as belonging to their own Judaistic faith. 'Not so!' the writer of the letter is saying in effect. 'The Old Testament belongs to the Christian church, because it points to Christ.' Charles

Jennens would have agreed wholeheartedly – and so should we. Many of the texts in Hebrews 1 are from the Book of Psalms. The writer introduces each of the quotations with the simple formula 'he says', referring clearly to God. There is no doubt in his mind that the Scriptures are the voice of God: whoever the human writer was in any of these Old Testament texts, their real author is God himself.

Movement 34 is a very short tenor recitative, and Jennens chooses for this item Hebrews 1:5a, the very first of this Bible chapter's selection of Old Testament texts. The quotation in this half-verse is from Psalm 2:7. As we have already seen, Psalm 2 is an important messianic psalm. (A fuller discussion of it will be left until Part II Scene 6, which makes use of verses 1–4 of Psalm 2.) Paul referred to Psalm 2:7 in his sermon at Antioch of Pisidia: he said that God had fulfilled what he promised to Old Testament Israel by raising Jesus and then quoted Psalm 2:7 in support of this. The thought seems to be that the 'begetting', spoken of in this psalm, was spiritually fulfilled in the resurrection (Acts 13:33).

Jennens leaves out the second half of Hebrews 1:5, which is the second of the Biblical writer's selected Old Testament texts, 'I will be to him a father, and he shall be to me a son' – this being a quotation from 2 Samuel 7:14, words spoken by God through Nathan to David, which we have already noted are to be understood as a promise that the Messiah would be a king born of David's line.

The next verse in Hebrews 1, verse 6, reads as follows: 'And again, when he brings the firstborn into the world, he says, "Let all God's angels worship him."' The term 'firstborn' may be an allusion to Psalm 89:27, referring to David or to his messianic offspring. But it is the end part of Hebrews 1:6 which Jennens chooses for the text of Movement 35. Here we find the third of the Biblical writer's selected Old Testament verses – this one apparently a quotation from the Greek Septuagint version of Deuteronomy 32:43.[1] That verse is part of the song of Moses, which looks ahead to the triumph of God over his adversaries. The Biblical writer transfers the triumph of God to the Messiah, whom he sees as God's 'firstborn', according to the first part of verse 6. The argument in Hebrews 1 is that the one whom the angels of God are to worship must be superior to them.

---

[1] See the NIV margin.

What to listen out for in the music in Part II Scene 4

34. Recitative: *'Unto which of the angels'*

A short recitative.

35. Chorus: *'Let all the angels of God worship him'*

This festive chorus in D major begins with the words of Hebrews 1:6b being sung in block chord style for the first few bars.

From then on, the words are sung in a contrapuntal style. The sopranos' opening phrase is repeated in its basic shape by the other voices in turn, but sometimes at double the speed (halving the note values). For the listener who notices this feature, the musical interest is increased.

The familiar ascending fourth appears at the beginning of the sopranos' first two phrases and in other parts in all four voices, as they imitate the sopranos' opening phrase.

Part II Scene 5: The Messiah's Mission Continues in the Preaching of the Gospel

36. Air (bass)
Thou art gone up on high, thou hast led captivity captive, and received gifts for men, yea, even for thine enemies, that the Lord God might dwell among them. (Psalm 68:18)

37. Chorus
The Lord gave the word: great was the company of the preachers. (Psalm 68:11)

38. Air (soprano)
How beautiful are the feet that preach the gospel of peace, and bring glad tidings of good things! (Romans 10:15b)

39. Chorus
Their sound is gone out into all lands, and their words unto the end of the world. (Psalm 19:4)

This scene and Acts 2

Jennens's title for this scene is 'Whitsun, the gift of tongues, the beginning of evangelism.' Here is a clear indication that he specifically had Acts 2 in mind: the remarkable events of the Day of Pentecost. 'Whitsun' is a word that is falling into disuse today and is largely replaced by the more Biblical term 'Pentecost'. Pentecost was already a major Jewish festival: originally the middle of the three annual Jewish harvest festivals, and also called the Feast of Weeks. It attracted thousands of adherents of the Jewish faith to Jerusalem from all nations of the known world. Luke tells us that it was on this day, 50 days after Jesus' resurrection (and therefore ten days after the Ascension), that the Holy Spirit was poured out on the 120 believers. As a result, they were empowered with 'the gift of tongues', in other words the supernatural ability to speak to an international audience in their own languages. They told 'the mighty works of God' (Acts 2:11), enabling these visitors to understand for themselves, without having to grapple with Hebrew or Aramaic, the good news of Jesus. The ensuing stir led to Peter's Pentecost sermon, in which he explained that the outpouring of the Holy Spirit was a fulfilment of Old Testament prophecy. Also it provided evidence that Jesus, whom they (the people of Jerusalem) had crucified – albeit 'according to the definite plan and foreknowledge of God' (Acts 2:23), – was risen and exaled. As a result of Peter's sermon, 3,000 people were converted that day.

So we can see that Jennens's intended scene title covers Acts 2 (Whitsun, the gift of tongues, the beginning of evangelism). But we may be puzzled that, at first sight, his choice of Bible texts hardly seems to have any direct connection with Acts 2. The theme of 'the beginning of evangelism' is certainly present in the text of Movements 37–39. But where, we may ask, is any reference to Pentecost or to the gift of the Holy Spirit? However, in a subtle way – again by imaginative use of mainly Old Testament texts – Jennens does make the connections between his title and his chosen Bible verses, as we shall see in the following discussion.

Gifts for ministry of the word (Psalm 68:18 and Ephesians 4:8)

Movement 36 is a contralto air with words from Psalm 68:18. The ESV rendering of this verse is:

> You ascended on high,
> leading a host of captives in your train
> and receiving gifts among men,
> even among the rebellious, that the Lord God may dwell there.

It is possible, although we cannot be certain, that Psalm 68 was written for the procession of the ark of the covenant, organised by David, from the house of Obed-Edom to the city of David, recorded in 2 Samuel 6. If this is the correct background to the psalm, it would make sense of the implied journey in the psalm: from 'God shall arise' (v 1), echoing the words with which the ark set out on all its journeys (Num 10:35), to 'the mount that God desired for his abode' (v 16) – in other words, Mount Zion. The theme of ascending is specifically mentioned in verse 18 of the psalm, and in the New Testament we find that Paul quotes this verse in Ephesians 4:8 with reference both to Christ's ascension and, because he focuses on the 'gifts' which Christ distributes, also implicitly to Pentecost.

The interesting feature of Paul's use of Psalm 68:18 in Ephesians 4:8 is that he changes 'receiving gifts among men' to 'gave gifts to men.' We may be surprised by Paul's decision to change the wording of the text. There are two helpful ways to meet this apparent difficulty:

- One is that the Targum (the Jewish Aramaic paraphrase) on the Psalms, which goes back to pre-Christian times, speaks of the *giving* rather than the *receiving* of gifts in this verse.
- The second is to refer to Acts 2:33, when Peter in his Pentecost sermon says, 'Being ... exalted at the right hand of God, and having *received* from the Father the promise of the Holy Spirit, he has *poured out* this' (my italics). There is a logical progression from the one to the other. Through his victory at Calvary he has conquered his enemies and returned to his Father's throne in triumph. From there he *gives* his blessings to his people. *'Receiving'* leads to *'giving'* (or 'pouring out'). In other words, Paul draws out the full Christian application of Psalm 68:18, but without doing damage to the integrity of the Old Testament text. What conquerors *took* from their captives, they *gave* to their followers.[1]

In the following verses of Ephesians 4, Paul elaborates on the gifts that the ascended Christ has given. In verse 11 he says, 'And he gave the apostles, the prophets, the evangelists, the pastors and teachers'. It is significant that Paul majors in this list on what we might call 'word gifts' – apostles and prophets, whose role was foundational to the New Testament church (Eph 2:20); evangelists, with the role of spreading the gospel (which is particularly relevant to the present discussion of this section of *Messiah*); and pastor-teachers, which we should take as a combined term applying to the leaders of local churches (synonymous therefore with the New Testament words 'elders' and 'overseers'). All these gifts of word-based ministries, ranging from the unique apostles (and those associated with them) who gave us the New Testament

---

[1] We find an illustration of this in the incident in the life of David, when he defeats the Amalekites who have plundered his current home-town of Ziklag and shares the spoils of his victory among his followers, including 200 of them whom he had left behind to guard the baggage (1 Sam 30).

Scriptures, to the pastor-teachers of every generation up to the present, are:

> to equip the saints (in other words, all Christians) for the work of ministry, for building up the body of Christ, until we all attain to the unity of the faith and of the knowledge of the Son of God, to mature manhood, to the measure of the stature of the fullness of Christ. (Eph 4:12–13)

The above discussion goes beyond the focus of Handel's oratorio, of course. But the inclusion of Ephesians 4:8 (and the following verses of that chapter) helps to establish the clear connection in Psalm 68:18 between 'Whitsun', 'the gift of tongues' and 'the beginning of evangelism'. The purpose of 'the gift of tongues' in Acts 2, as we have seen, was to equip those first Christians to preach the gospel, and this is also the case with the 'word gifts' of Ephesians 4:11.

The preaching of the gospel (Psalm 68:11)

Movement 37 is a chorus with the text taken from another verse in Psalm 68, this time verse 11. In the context of the unfolding drama of this scene of *Messiah,* the words (taken from the *Book of Common Prayer* version) would seem to be very appropriate. They conjure up the picture of a vast number of *'preachers'* – or ministers, missionaries, Christian workers (the way the task of communicating the gospel in today's world goes under many names) – all obediently responding to the literally God-given word they seek to pass on to others.

Historically, such a statement is an accurate concise summary of the growth of the Christian church throughout the past 2,000 years. We think of the Book of Acts with its programmatic chapter 1 verse 8, spoken by the risen Christ to the original group of disciples: 'But you will receive power when the Holy Spirit has come upon you, and you will be my witnesses in Jerusalem and in all Judea and Samaria, and to the end of the earth.' Those widening concentric circles map out the content of what actually happened in the Book of Acts, as the gospel overcame the massive barriers which separated Jews from Samaritans, and Jews from Gentiles – so that, geographically, the book takes us from Jerusalem in chapter 1 to Rome, the capital of all that is represented by 'the end of the earth', in chapter 28. On the way, the 120 believers (Acts 1:15) grew to 3,000 (Acts 2:41), then to 5,000 (Acts 4:4), and beyond that further growth continued (Acts 6:7; etc).

Particularly relevant within the Book of Acts to the theme of *'great was the company of the preachers'* is the comment that those who were scattered throughout the regions of Judea and Samaria as a result of the persecution that followed Stephen's martyrdom 'went about preaching the word' (Acts 8:4). This is ordinary Christians passing on the gospel. A few chapters later, Luke tells us that some who were scattered as a result of the persecution after Stephen's death travelled as far as Phoenicia, Cyprus and Antioch (this is the Antioch in Syria). Initially, this outreach was to Jews only, but then in Antioch it spread to 'the Hellenists', meaning Greek-speaking Gentiles. This led to the planting of the church in Antioch, which was made up of believing Jews and Gentiles (Acts 11:19–26) and which became a major sending church in the further spread of the Christian gospel in the early decades of the church (see, for example, Acts 13:1–3). Michael Green spells out the importance of the achievement of these first-century Christians and the example they set for all subsequent generations. He says that the:

> enthusiasm to evangelize which marked the early Christians is one of the most remarkable things in the history of religion. Men and women of every walk of life were so sure that they had the answer to their religious problems that they let nothing stand in the way of passing on good news to others.[2]

Gospel outreach has always been to the fore of the Christian church when it has been true to its calling. 'The church exists by mission as fire exists by burning', wrote Emil Brunner, and every generation of Christians needs to be reminded of this truth.[3] Today in particular, when political correctness tries to gag the proclamation of the gospel in the name of a pluralistic relativism, ordinary Christians must take heart and follow the

---

[2] E. M. B. Green, *Evangelism in the Early Church* (London: Hodder and Stoughton, 1970), 286.

[3] H. E. Brunner, *The Word and the World* (London: SCM Press, 1931), 11.

bold examples of believers in the early church and in recent centuries. Lesslie Newbigin was right when he made this statement:

> The Church does not apologise for the fact that it wants all men to know Jesus Christ and to follow him. Its very calling is to proclaim the Gospel to the ends of the earth. It cannot make any restrictions in this respect.[4]

The previous paragraphs most certainly represent what we should understand Charles Jennens to have had in mind in this movement. However, there is one problem that should be mentioned. The *Book of Common Prayer* version of Psalm 68:11, which is essentially the same as in the AV (and the NIV follows its lead), may conjure up the picture of eager, trained preachers leaving theological college or Bible college and ready for parish-ministry or the mission-field. But a more accurate translation of the verse is provided by the ESV: 'The Lord gives the word; the women who announce the news are a great host.'

Charles Jennens, and others like him whose staple diet was the *Book of Common Prayer* and the Authorised Version, would probably not have realised that the word for 'those that published' the word (AV) or 'the preachers' (*Book of Common Prayer*) is feminine – as the ESV makes clear. In the celebration that accompanies the procession of the ark to its new resting place (if that is indeed the background to the psalm), women are encouraged to take up the news of God's triumph with songs and dances, as happened in 1 Samuel 18:6, following David's earlier victories.

Does this understanding of the more precise meaning of Psalm 68:11 detract from our appreciation of this part of Handel's *Messiah*? As on an earlier occasion in this book, our answer again has to be a 'yes' and a 'no':

- 'Yes': we should seek to maintain integrity and accuracy in our use of Scripture, "rightly handling (or dividing) the word of truth" (2 Tim.2:15). It may be questioned if that is really the case here. The word "preachers," taken from the Book of

[4] Cited in J. Young, *Our God Is Still Too Small* (London: Hodder and Stoughton, 1988), 155.

Common Prayer version of Psalm 68.11, implies more than the original text is really saying.

- On the other hand, a case can be made for a 'no' as the answer to the above question. Psalm 68:11, with or without its specific gender-reference, provides a useful statement of Christian mission ahead of its times. To a certain extent, the women of Psalm 68:11 who are envisaged in announcing the good news are a reminder of the truth commented on above that, in the Book of Acts, it was ordinary Christians – and by implication women just as much as men – who were actively passing on the gospel (Acts 8:4). And the instructions of Colossians 4:5-6 and 1 Peter 3:15 apply to all Christians. In the words of Eric Liddell, the famous Olympic gold medallist and missionary to China, 'We are all missionaries ... Wherever we go, we either bring people nearer to Christ, or we repel them from Christ. We are working for the great Kingdom of God.'[5]

Preaching the gospel of peace (Romans 10:15 and Isaiah 52:7)

Movement 38 is a lovely soprano air with words from the second half of Romans 10:15, which are themselves a direct quotation by the apostle Paul from Isaiah 52:7. Jennens chooses to use the AV rendering of the New Testament quotation rather than the original words in Isaiah but, once again, we are made aware of the way Jennens was drawn towards Old Testament texts to emphasise New Testament truth. It will be helpful to look at both these verses.

Isaiah 52:7 in the ESV reads as follows:

> How beautiful upon the mountains are the feet of him
> who brings good news,
> who publishes peace,
> who brings good news of happiness,
> who publishes salvation,
> who says to Zion, 'Your God reigns.'

---

[5] Cited in D. McCasland, *Eric Liddell: Pure Gold* (Oxford: Lion Hudson plc, 2012), 159.

To a modern ear, to call someone's feet 'beautiful' sounds strange, but the Good News Bible expresses the opening of this verse with great freshness: 'How wonderful it is to see a messenger coming across the mountains, bringing good news.' We can imagine how the people's anxious waiting changes to exuberant joy as it become clear that this man – possibly breathless but bursting with excitement – is the bearer of 'good news'. The content of his 'good news' is unpacked in four phrases.

- First, he announces 'peace', which – in the terms of the picture – suggests news from a battle. The reality of the picture is far more momentous: this 'peace' is the end of God's wrath, which has been described in Isaiah 51:17–23.
- Secondly, the messenger announces 'good news of happiness', which more literally is 'good news of good' – the sheer goodness of the good news is beyond words.
- Thirdly, the messenger announces 'salvation', namely God's victory over every enemy and the end of sin's oppression.
- And fourthly, the messenger announces, 'Your God reigns.' In the following verse of Isaiah's prophecy (Isa 52:8) there is the joyful prospect of seeing the return of the Lord in person, 'eye to eye', which means 'with their own eyes'.

In earlier discussions, we have considered parts of Isaiah 40 (Part I Scene 1) and Isaiah 53 (Part II Scene 1). It will be evident that the good news of the messenger of Isaiah 52:7 is closely connected with the Messiah himself, who is coming in person to save his people and to announce the reality of peace with God, because he has turned from his wrath against the sins of his people. Here, as in chapter 40, is the assurance of 'comfort' for God's people, the end of their 'warfare' and the pardon of their 'iniquity.' Chapter 53, as we have seen, tells us what brings about this 'good news:' the substitutionary death of the Suffering Servant, whom we know to be none other than the Messiah, taking on himself his people's guilt and judgement in full.

At this stage in the oratorio, as will be evident from the discussion of the last few pages, what Charles Jennens has in mind is the message of this good news being taken into the whole world following the victorious events of the first Good Friday and Easter Day. The topic of worldwide evangelism is most definitely the context of Romans 10:15, which is Paul's slightly curtailed quotation of the first part of Isaiah 52:7. Chapters 1 to 8 of Romans are Paul's breathtaking exposition of the gospel message of justification and assurance, and chapters 9 to 11 tackle the problems raised by large-scale unbelief on the part of the Jewish people. Given that the gospel had been 'promised beforehand through the prophets in the holy Scriptures' (Rom 1:2) – and the libretto of this oratorio illustrates the truth of this statement – why is it that Jewish people of those early decades of the Christian era have been so unresponsive? It is beyond the scope of this discussion to explore all that Paul has to say in Romans 9 to 11 about God's purpose of election, Israel's present disobedience and what Paul describes as Israel's future salvation, but we focus for now on Romans 10:14–15, where Paul touches on the necessity of evangelism.

It is the abiding truth of God's word that 'everyone who calls on the name of the Lord will be saved' (Rom 10:17). This is a quotation from Joel 2:32, which Peter made use of in his Pentecost sermon (Acts 2:21). Whatever else may need to be said about God's election and human disobedience, nothing takes away from the need for Christian believers to press on with the work of gospel-evangelism.

Paul asks four connected questions, in order to demonstrate how indispensable evangelism is within God's purposes for salvation:

- 'How then will they call on him in whom they have not believed?' (v 14a) – given that sinners must call on the name of the Lord to be saved (v 13), that calling on the Lord must be the result of believing the promise of his Word.
- 'How are they to believe in him of whom they have never heard?' (v 14b) – the message needs to be brought to them.
- 'How are they to hear without someone preaching?' (v 14c) – the image is of the herald publicly proclaiming the message.
- 'How are they to preach unless they are sent?' (v 15a) – missionaries or evangelists or preachers need to be sent for this purpose.

It is at this point in the argument (Rom 10:15) that Paul confirms the need for 'heralds' from Old Testament Scripture by quoting from Isaiah 52:7: *'How beautiful are the feet that preach the gospel of peace, and bring glad tidings of good things!'* The arrival of that lone messenger in Isaiah's prophecy, coming across the mountains with his message of the good news of the end of exile, would have been welcomed with great joy. How much more glorious must be the fulfilment of that prophecy in terms of Christian heralds proclaiming the release of spiritual exiles from the captivity of sin!

Worldwide proclamation (Psalm 19:4 and Romans 10:18)

Movement 39 is a chorus with words from Psalm 19:4. In their Old Testament context, *'their sound'* refers to the witness of 'the heavens' – in other words, the stars of the universe as seen on a clear, moonless night without the interference of street lamps – which speak volumes of God's creative power and majesty. As verse 1 of the psalm puts it, 'The heavens declare the glory of God, and the sky above proclaims his handiwork' – we may be familiar with the setting of those words in Haydn's oratorio *The Creation*. Their witness is a silent one: 'there is no speech, nor are there words, whose voice is not heard' (v 3). And yet, 'their measuring line (as ESV renders it: the more familiar 'their voice' – or *'their sound'* – is a reading of the Septuagint) goes out through all the earth, and their words to the ends of the world' (Ps 19:4). These verses from the beginning of Psalm 19 make the same point that Paul spells out in Romans 1, speaking of those whose wickedly suppress the truth of God's revelation:

> For what can be known about God is plain to them, because God has shown it to them. For his invisible attributes, namely his eternal power and divine nature, have been clearly perceived, ever since the creation of the world, in the things that have been made (Rom 1:19–20).

While the above paragraph sets Psalm 19:4 in its Scriptural context as a statement about God's revelation of his glory in the wonders of the universe, clearly Jennens's intention in this movement is to make a statement about the worldwide proclamation of the gospel. *'Their sound'*, the first words of the chorus, are made to appear to refer to *'them that preach the gospel of peace'* in the previous movement. But Jennens is on sure ground in his selection of this particular text, because the apostle Paul himself makes use of Psalm 19:4 with reference to gospel proclamation, and he does so in the very same passage of Scripture that we were discussing in the previous movement, namely Romans 10.

Paul has been arguing for the necessity of evangelism in God's purposes of salvation, as we have seen. 'But', he says, 'they [in other words, Jewish people] have not all obeyed the gospel' (Rom 10:16a), although they should have done so. Indeed, 'faith comes from hearing, and hearing through the word of Christ' (Rom 10:17). 'Have they not heard?' Paul asks, and answers his own question, 'Indeed they have' (Rom 10:18a), substantiating this fact by quoting Psalm 19:4:

> for
> Their voice has gone out to all the earth,
> and their words to the ends of the world' (Rom 10:18b)

Paul's choice of this Bible quotation may appear to us somewhat surprising. After all, as we have seen, Psalm 19 is about God's revelation of his glory in creation, not the worldwide spread of the gospel. But Paul quotes it as if it is referring to worldwide gospel proclamation. Paul quite deliberately transfers the Bible's own language about global witness from creation to the church. Surprising as Paul's use of the Old Testament is at this point, it is also appropriate. The message of the glory of the *new* creation must be spread no less widely than the message of the glory of God's *original* creation.

We may wish to raise the question whether it is true that the gospel 'has gone out to all the earth'. Is it not the case, as the often quoted phrase puts it, that 'Untold millions are still untold'?[6] Has it ever been true that the gospel has spread worldwide? Was it true when Paul wrote his letter to the Romans? Those questions lead to further ones to do with our approach to these Bible verses. Is Psalm 19:4 (applied by Paul to gospel outreach) to be viewed as an understandable hyperbole? Or is the meaning that the gospel had already been announced to virtually every

---

[6] Quoted by Rev. Derrick Lau in *Harvestforce* (The Methodist Missions Society, Singapore, 2019), Issue 1, 2.

community in the Mediterranean world where there were Jews? In view of Paul's missionary endeavours (and those of others first century Christians), this could well have been the case.

However we respond to these questions, it is clear that for us today the words of Psalm 19:4, *'Their sound is gone out into all lands, and their words unto the end of the world',* can never be used as an excuse for complacency. The task is never complete and must be tackled afresh in each generation. The Great Commission of the risen Christ to 'go ... and make disciples of all nations' (Matt 28:19) remains as valid today as it ever has been.

What to listen out for in the music in Part II Scene 5

36. Air: *'Thou art gone up on high'*

Listeners should not be surprised if it is not the bass soloist who sings it, as indicated at the beginning of this scene, but one of the other voices. As was explained in the Introduction, there is nothing strange about a different voice singing a particular item.

37. Chorus: *'The Lord gave the word'*

One interesting feature of the music for this chorus is that the words of the Bible verse are stated twice, and both times in such a way as to emphasise the contrast between the two halves of the verse: the Lord's command, and the obedient response of *'the preachers'*.

The first time, the tenors and the basses – in unison and unaccompanied – sing, *'The Lord gave the word'*, in the key of Bb major, followed by all voices singing the words *'great was the company of the preachers'* with repetitions and long *coloraturas* on *'company'*. The second time, the sopranos and contraltos sing, *'The Lord gave the word'*, again in unison and unaccompanied, and in the related key of F major, before all parts join in with the second part of the text and return to the home key of Bb.

38. Air: *'How beautiful are the feet'*

This soprano air is a particularly engaging item – one to be enjoyed for its lovely tune.

39. Chorus: *'Their sound is gone out into all lands'*

A contrapuntal style is used throughout this chorus. As each voice enters in turn with its initial *'Their sound is gone out'*, the effect is to intensify the impression of the multiplicity of witnesses taking the gospel message *'into all lands ... unto the ends of the world'*.

Part II Scene 6: The Messiah's Rejection by the World

40. Air (bass)
Why do the nations so furiously rage together, and why do the people imagine a vain thing? The kings of the earth rise up, and the rulers take counsel together against the Lord and against his anointed. (Psalm 2:1–2)

41. Chorus
Let us break their bonds asunder, and cast away their yokes from us. (Psalm 2:3)

42. Recitative (tenor)
He that dwelleth in heaven shall laugh them to scorn: the Lord shall have them in derision. (Psalm 2:4)

Opposition to the gospel

Charles Jennens's original title for this scene is 'The world and its rulers reject the gospel.' It is an appropriate theme to include at this point in the developing drama of the oratorio, for the Book of Acts records not only the unstoppable advance of the gospel, as we have seen in the discussion of the previous scene, as it overcame all sorts of barriers and spreads from Jerusalem to Rome, in accordance with Jesus' promise and instructions of Acts 1:8. But also Acts records the relentless opposition from the authorities, particularly the Jewish hierarchy and, later, those bitterly opposed to Paul's preaching of a gospel of grace to Gentiles as well as to Jews. Even though the Council of Jerusalem in 49 AD ratified the full inclusion of Gentile believers within the Christian church (Acts 15), Luke nevertheless focuses particularly on the opposition experienced by Paul in this regard. From Acts 2 onwards, when some people mocked the Christian believers' multilingual proclamation of the gospel as drunken babbling (Acts 2:13), there is hardly a chapter in Acts which does not include some reference to opposition.

The history of the church over the past 2,000 years is a record of both the spread of Christianity across the world and of opposition, often fierce, from those hostile to the gospel message. One thinks of the persecutions by Roman emperors such as Domitian, Decius and Diocletian; the suppression of the Lollards, the followers of John Wyclif; the violent deaths of Reformers in the reign of Queen Mary I; and much else besides. During the twentieth century, more Christians were martyred than in all the previous centuries added together. Today, in many parts of the world, Christian believers pay a high price – ostracism, harassment, beatings, death – for their Christian witness. Even in our less violent United Kingdom, those who speak openly of their Christian faith are increasingly vilified and victimised in the name of a political correctness which is opposed to the teaching of the Bible.

All four Gospels spell out the mounting opposition to Jesus during the time of his ministry, leading eventually to his crucifixion. We also find Jesus warning his disciples of the opposition that they too would experience. In Matthew 10, for example, before sending out the twelve apostles on a mission, he alerts them of what lies ahead in terms which seem to go far beyond the immediate mission to 'the lost sheep of the house of Israel' (Matt 10:6):

> Behold, I am sending you out as sheep in the midst of wolves, so be wise as serpents and innocent as doves. Beware of men, for they will deliver you over to courts and flog you in their synagogues, and you will be dragged before governors and kings for my sake, to bear witness before them and the Gentiles (Matt 10:16–18).

Another significant instance of Jesus warning his disciples of what lay ahead occurs in John 15 and 16 – teaching given on the evening before the crucifixion:

> If the world hates you, know that it has hated me before it hated you ... Remember the word that I said to you: 'A servant is not greater than his master.' If they persecuted me, they will also persecute you ... They will put you out of the synagogues. Indeed, the hour is coming when whoever kills you will think he is offering service to God ... In the world you will have

> tribulation. But take heart; I have overcome the world (John 15:18, 20; 16:2, 33).

From this brief survey of opposition to the gospel, as foretold by Jesus and experienced by the early church and the church down the ages, we should take note that it all takes place within the sovereign purposes of God. That is the encouraging truth to be derived from the last of the above quoted verses of Jesus from John 16:33, namely that his followers can take heart when they face the world's tribulations because he has overcome the world. Jesus promises elsewhere that he will build his church and the gates of Hades shall not prevail against it (Matt 16:18) and that he will be with his followers in their proclamation of the gospel throughout the whole world until the end of time (Matt 28:18–20).

As we now look at the handling of the theme of the world's opposition in this scene of *Messiah,* we find that Jennens's choice of texts rightly reflects this Biblical perspective of God's sovereignty over all opposition.

The world's opposition against God and his Messiah (Psalm 2:1–3)

This scene is made up of four consecutive verses from the same Bible passage – Psalm 2:1–4. The first movement of the next scene uses one further verse from the same psalm. Psalm 2 is much quoted in the New Testament, where it is clearly recognised as a messianic psalm. It has been referred to a few times already in this book. In this section we look at verses 1–3 which deal with the world's opposition. Verse 4, to which we will turn in a moment, deals with God's response.

Movement 40 is a bass air with the words taken from verses 1 and 2 of the psalm. *'Why?'* powerfully expresses the sense of astonishment that *'the nations'* should reject God's rule and *'his anointed'*, in other words, the Messiah whom he has appointed. Verse 6 of this psalm tell us that this Messiah is none other than God's appointed King, and verse 7 that he is God's begotten Son (this latter verse is quoted in Hebrews 1:5, and we met it in Movement 34 in the previous scene but one). This rejection of their rightful ruler is akin to the attitude of the citizens in Jesus' parable of the Ten Minas. They send a delegation after the nobleman who has gone to secure his nomination as king – clearly representing none other than Jesus – and they say 'We do not want this man to reign over us'

(Luke 19:14). The rebellion of the world and its *'kings'* and *'rulers'* is utterly senseless and is doomed to failure: it is *'a vain thing'* that they *'imagine'* – ESV has 'plot' for this last word, which carries the idea of murmuring.

One particular New Testament use of Psalm 2:1–2 occurs in Acts 4:25–26 and clearly illustrates the strong sense of God's sovereignty conveyed by these words of Scripture. The two verses in Acts 4 come as part of the prayer of the apostles and their friends following the release of Peter and John, who had been arrested by the Jewish authorities. This had come about as a result of Peter's bold preaching about the Risen Christ to the crowd who had witnessed the miraculous healing of a lame man in the temple precincts. In their prayer in Acts 4 the Christian believers acknowledge God as Sovereign Lord and in support of this truth they quote the two verses from Psalm 2. But they go on to apply this Scripture to Herod and Pontius Pilate, "along with the Gentiles and the people of Israel," in gathering together against Jesus, the one whom God "anointed" and yet whose death was "predestined" by God (Acts 4:27-28). Significantly, instead of praying for safety from further danger, the Christian believers ask God to "look upon their threats and grant to your servants to continue to speak your word with all boldness" (Acts 4:29).

Nothing can demonstrate the sovereignty of God more clearly than the Cross of Christ. From one perspective, the death of his Son was carried out by wicked men and approved of by the crowd who cried, "Crucify him!" But from the divine perspective, it was the means that God had "predestined" for the salvation of the world. The very worst that mankind could devise brought about the very best that God had always intended.

Church history is punctuated by demonstrations of the abiding truth of God's sovereignty in circumstances which at first sight might appear to be setbacks for the cause of the gospel. Two out of many possible instances are included here.

One concerns the martyrdom of two prominent Reformers, Hugh Latimer and Nicholas Ridley, in 1555, during the reign of Mary Tudor. They were burned at the stake together in Oxford. Among the final words spoken by the two men were those spoken by Latimer: 'Be of good comfort, Master Ridley, and play the man. We shall this day light such a candle by God's grace in England as I trust shall never be put out!'[1] The courageous faith of such men did indeed light such a candle and has put backbone into many a generation of those who have inherited their evangelical convictions and their concern for the spread of the gospel.

The second instance highlighted here concerns five young American Christian men (Jim Elliot, Pete Fleming, Nate Saint, Ed McCully and Roger Youderian), working with Missionary Aviation Fellowship and known afterwards as the 'Mid-Century Martyrs.' In 1956, they lost their lives in an attempt to bring the gospel to the Auca Indians in the Amazon forests of South America. They were killed by the very people they were trying to reach.[2] One of the results of that event was that the wife of one of the men and the sister of another (Elisabeth Elliot and Rachel Saint) went back to the Auca Indians, and many of them were converted. Another result was the very high number of men who, year after year for the next decade or so, offered themselves for missionary service. Both these incidents, chosen out of many similar ones, illustrate the truth of Paul's comment on his sufferings recorded in the later chapters of Acts: 'I want you to know, brothers, that what has happened to me has really served to advance the gospel' (Phil 1:12).

Movement 41 is a chorus, using words from Psalm 2:3. The irony of the nations' complaint against God is that, while they view the rule of God and his Messiah as *'bonds'* and *'yokes'*, God's purpose for his people is to lead them with 'cords of kindness' (Hosea 11:4) and to lay upon them a yoke that is 'easy' and a burden that is 'light' (Matt 11:29–30).

As a technical comment, whereas both the *Book of Common Prayer* and the AV have the word 'cords' in the second half of verse 3, Jennens has deliberately replaced it with the word *'yokes'*, possibly in order to suggest a deliberate contrast with the 'yoke' of Matthew 11:29–30, which he has already made use of in Movements 20 and 21.

God's derisive laughter (Psalm 2:4)

Movement 42 is a very short tenor recitative, with the soloist singing the words of verse 4 of Psalm 2, following on from the Bible text of the

[1] Stephen Cattley, *The Acts and Monuments of John Foxe,* (London: R.R. Seeley and W. Burnside, 1841) Vol VII, 550.
[2] E. Elliot, *Through Gates of Splendour* (Bromley: Send The Light, 1980).

previous scene. Here is God's response to mankind's rebellion: the one who sits on the throne of heaven *'shall laugh them to scorn'* and *'have them in derision'.* The following two verses of the Psalm go on to tell us that 'he will speak to them in his wrath and terrify them in his fury' (Ps 2:5) and that he will announce that, regardless of their opposition, he has enthroned his King (the Messiah) on Zion (Ps 2:6). Subsequent verses in the psalm spell out God's purposes that his King (who is none other than his Son) shall rule the nations (Ps 2:7–8).

What to listen out for in the music in Part II Scene 6

40. Air: *'Why do the nations so furiously rage together'*

This bass air is in C major, accompanied by an orchestra in continuous motion, portraying the seething turmoil of the rebellious nations of the world.

The word *'rage'* is expressed by a long *melisma* of triplets, conveying a feeling of agitation.

41. Chorus: *'Let us break their bonds asunder'*

It is appropriate for this item to be a chorus rather than a solo, as verse 3 of Psalm 2 expresses the words of the nations and their rulers.

Much of the movement is in contrapuntal style, so the different voices coming in at different times with the same words, *'Let us break their bonds asunder',* etc., intensify the impression of a great number of individuals participating in the world's rebellion against God and his Messiah.

42. Recitative: *'He that dwelleth in heaven shall laugh them to scorn'*

Another short recitative.

Part II Scene 7: The Messiah's Victory

43. **Air (tenor)**
Thou shalt break them with a rod of iron; thou shalt dash them in pieces like a potter's vessel. (Psalm 2:9)
44. **Chorus**
Hallelujah, for the Lord God Omnipotent reigneth.
The kingdom of this world is become the kingdom of our Lord and of his Christ; and he shall reign for ever and ever.
King of kings, and Lord of lords. (Revelation 19:6b, 11:15b, 19:16b)

The Messiah's triumph over all opposition: Psalm 2:9

Movement 43 is an air for the tenor with yet another verse from Psalm 2.[1] We need to bear in mind that it is God who speaks these words and that the one who will *'break'* the nations *'with a rod of iron'* and will *'dash them to pieces like a potter's vessel'*, is the Lord's anointed, who is Jesus. This means that the popular and sentimental picture of 'gentle Jesus, meek and mild' has to be challenged. Of course, there is a gentleness and meekness in Jesus' tender compassion to his needy people, as we saw in the earlier discussion of Part I Scene 5, and particularly in Jesus' invitation to 'all who labour and are heavy laden' to come to him in Matthew 11:28–30. But the truth being spelt out in Psalm 2:9 is that Jesus will ultimately triumph over all opposition. The Book of Revelation quotes these words three times, once concerning the victorious Christian (Rev 2:27) – this indicates that Christian believers are promised a share in the reign of Christ in the age to come – and twice concerning Jesus (Rev 12:5 and 19:15).[2]

---

[1] Jennens uses the AV reading of Psalm 2:9 rather than the *Book of Common Prayer* version, which he normally prefers in his rendering of verses from the Book of Psalms.

[2] The footnote in the ESV for Psalm 2:9 indicates that a revocalisation of the Hebrew word for 'you shall break' yields 'you shall rule' (or 'shepherd'), which is the reading followed by the Greek Septuagint and the three quotations of this verse in Revelation.

Hallelujah (Revelation 11 and 19)

Movement 44, the 'Hallelujah' Chorus, must rank as the most popular single item in the whole oratorio and one of the best known pieces of music of all time. It is reported that Handel's servant found him in tears when working on this movement and exclaiming, 'I did think I did see heaven before me and the great God himself seated on His throne, with the company of Angels..'[3]

There is a popular story that King George II, attending a performance of *Messiah,* was so moved by the 'Hallelujah' Chorus that he rose to his feet and remained standing until the last chords. It goes without saying that, if the monarch stands up, all those in his presence will likewise stand up. The tradition of standing during the 'Hallelujah' Chorus continues to this day. This account of the origin of the tradition of standing for this movement is disputed by some, and if it is true, the jury is out on whether the king was simply moved by the music or felt compelled to stand in the presence of the *'King of kings and Lord of lords'.* There are those who make a point of remaining seated at performances, and it is true that no tradition can fail to be challenged. Some will say that we honour Jesus by living for him with all our lives, not by standing for a piece of music. My view is that, if it is possibly true that King George II made a point of standing as an act of acknowledgement of a far greater king, I for one do not want to be left behind in standing up for Jesus – both during the 'Hallelujah' Chorus and in the whole of my life.

The 'Hallelujah' Chorus is a magnificent climax to the second part of the oratorio. Having traced the career of Jesus Christ from Old Testament promise of his coming to a survey of his birth, ministry, sufferings, death, resurrection, ascension – followed by the proclamation of the gospel throughout the world – and then on to his ultimate triumph over all opposition, what can the next stage in the unfolding drama be? One answer might be: Christ's second coming, which is by no means a minor doctrine and is clearly taught by every New Testament author. However, Jennens's libretto includes no specific reference to the Last Day (except perhaps implicitly in Part I Scene 2, where the note of judgement

---

[3] Horatio Townsend, 'An Account of the Visit of Handel to Dublin' (1852) citing Laetitia Matilda Hawkins, 'Anecdotes, Biographical Sketches and Memoirs' vol. 1 (1822).

announced there will only find its true fulfilment on the day of Christ's return). We can only speculate why this is so. My guess (and that is all it is) would be that Jennens's instincts led him to see the next stage of the drama as heaven itself. So, with the superlative skills of Handel to provide a fitting musical framework, he takes us to the throne of God in order to join in this masterpiece of praise and adoration.

The words are taken from three verses of Revelation. Here are the relevant verses as they appear in the ESV:

> Hallelujah! For the Lord our God the Almighty reigns (Rev 19:6b)
>
> The kingdom of the world has become the kingdom of our Lord and of his Christ, and he shall reign for ever and ever (Rev 11:15b)
>
> King of kings and Lord of lords (Rev 19:16b)

We shall take each of the three half-verses in turn.

'Hallelujah' is the key word of this chorus and it means 'Praise the Lord!'[4] *'Hallelujah'* is sung approximately 40 times by each of the four voices in the movement, and its repeated use powerfully and exuberantly reinforces the atmosphere of praise. The Book of Revelation has a cyclical structure, with repeated overviews of the whole course of history from Christ's first coming through to his second coming. But chapter 19, from which the first and third of the extracts of this movement are taken, looks forward to the climactic end of all things.

Four times in this chapter the cry 'Hallelujah' is voiced. The first time is in verse 1, as 'the loud voice of a great multitude in heaven' shouts 'Hallelujah!' in praise of God's just judgement on 'Babylon', which has oppressed God's people. The second time is in verse 3, as the same multitude repeats their praise to God for his triumph. The third time is the end of verse 4, with the 'Hallelujah!' coming from the twenty-four elders and the four living creatures. The fourth time – which is the first

[4] 'Hallelujah' is a transliteration of the Hebrew and is found in the AV margin for 'Praise ye the Lord' several times in the Book of Psalms (for example, Psalm 105:45). 'Alleluia' is a transliteration of the Greek and is the form used the four times in Revelation 19 in the AV.

of our half-verses of this movement – it is the cry of 'what seemed to be the voice of a great multitude, like the roar of many waters and like the sound of mighty peals of thunder', praising God for the marriage of the Lamb (a title for Christ). This *'Hallelujah!'* is followed by the words in this movement, *'for the Lord God Omnipotent reigneth.'* An old chorus used to be sung with the words, 'God is still on the throne.'[5] Indeed, with that assurance, the fiercest opposition, such as we have met in the previous movement, must fail.

The second extract from Revelation in this movement comes from 11:15. At this point in the book, the seventh angel blows his trumpet and loud voices in heaven utter the words, *'The kingdom of the world is become the kingdom of our Lord and of his Christ, and he shall reign for ever and ever.'* Within the cyclical structure of Revelation, we meet a number of sequences of seven. Each time, the seventh of the series looks forward to the grand climax of heaven to come, when the full extent of the rule of the Lord God and of his Messiah, which covers the all creation, will be finally and fully revealed. Even now Christian believers can be assured of the truth of Jesus' words, 'All authority in heaven and earth has been given to me' (Matt 28:18). Today, surrounded as we are by the furious raging of the nations and their rulers (once again we are reminded of the words of Psalm 2 in the previous scene), we can have full confidence that one day the full extent of God's sovereign rule will be clearly evident for all to see. In the words of Abraham Kuyper, 'There is not a square inch in the whole domain of our human existence over which Christ, who is Sovereign over all, does not cry: "Mine!"'[6]

For the third extract from Revelation in this movement, we return to chapter 19, this time to verse 16. At this point a truly impressive figure has made his entrance: a rider on a white horse (Rev 19:11–16). Although he is not named in these verses, there cannot be the slightest doubt that this is the Lord Jesus Christ. Descriptions are applied to him, such as his eyes being like flames of fire and a sharp sword coming from his mouth, which are reminiscent of the appearance of the risen and glorified Christ in John's vision in chapter 1 (verses 14 and 16). Revelation 19:15 tells us

[5] Mrs F. W Suffield, 'God is Still on the Throne', in *Scripture Union Songs and Choruses* (London: Scripture Union, 1982) No. 325.
[6] Cited in J.D. Bratt (ed.), *A Centennial Reader* (Grand Rapids: Eerdmans, 1998), 488.

more about the sharp sword coming from his mouth, namely that with it he will 'strike down the nations, and he will rule them with a rod of iron' (here is one of those quotations of Psalm 2:9 in the Book of Revelation, which was referred to in the discussion of the previous movement). Another significant description is his robe dipped in blood, pointing to his victorious sacrificial death on the cross. But also three titles are applied to Christ: 'Faithful and True' (v 11), 'The Word of God' (v 13 – with echoes of John 1), and – the words used in this movement – *'King of kings and Lord of lords'* (v 16).

Whether or not the story of King George II standing up during this movement is correct, the right response of any earthly ruler is to show this ruler of rulers due honour and respect – and the right response not only of earthly rulers but also of all their subjects.

In an essay, William Hazlitt records that, while Charles Lamb[7] was entertaining some friends, they began to talk about great figures of history and what they would do if one of these were to enter the room. Eventually the name of Jesus was mentioned, and there was a pause in the conversation. Charles Lamb said:

> If Shakespeare was to come into the room, we should all rise up to meet him. But if that Person were to come into it, we should all fall down and try to kiss the hem of His garment.[8]

Whether it is standing up (like George II possibly, or possibly not) or falling down (like Charles Lamb – and indeed the twenty-four elders and the four living creatures of Revelation 19:4) does not really matter. Responding rightly to the one who rules as Sovereign over all *does* matter, and doing it now in this life before it is too late.

---

[7] English essayist and poet (1775-1834).

[8] Cited in J.N.D. Anderson, *Jesus Christ: The Witness of History* (Leicester: Inter-Varsity Press, 1985), 46.

What to listen out for in the music in Part II Scene 7

43. Air: *'Thou shalt break them with a rod of iron'*

This is a forceful air, which well expresses God's power against his enemies.

44. Chorus: *'Hallelujah'*

There are a number of features of Handel's music in this famous chorus to comment on.

The key is D major, which is sometimes described as being the most radiant of keys and which we have met a few times already in the oratorio in triumphant movements. It is certainly well suited to the trumpets, which make their first proper appearance in this movement. In the earlier discussion on *'Glory to God'* (Movement 17 in Part I) it was noted that they were originally scored as *da lontano,* in other words, 'from a distance', playing off stage. In this movement they are joined by the timpani for the first time.

The choir introduces in block chord style a characteristic simple motif on the word *'Hallelujah',* which reappears throughout the piece.

The three extracts from Revelation, which were discussed above, are treated differently but are unified by *'Hallelujah'* as a conclusion or as a countersubject in a fugal section.

In the first extract the line *'for the Lord God omnipotent reigneth'* is sung by all voices, first in unison, then in imitation with Hallelujah-exclamations interspersed.

The second extract, *'The kingdom of this world'* is sung in a four-part setting like a chorale. The last part of this extract, *'and he shall reign for ever',* starts as a fugue on a theme with bold leaps. As a countersubject, the words *'for ever – and ever'* assume the rhythm of the Hallelujah motif.

The third extract, consisting of the acclamation *'King of kings',* is sung on one note, energised by repeated calls of *'Hallelujah'* and *'for ever – and ever',* raised higher and higher, and another famous 'Handelian hiatus' precedes the final triumphant 'Hallelujah!'

Part III: From death to life

Part III Scene 1: The Messiah's victory means the resurrection of the body – 1

45. Air (soprano)
I know that my redeemer liveth, and that he shall stand at the latter day upon the earth.
And though worms destroy this body, yet in my flesh shall I see God. (Job 19:25–26)
For now is Christ risen from the dead, the firstfruits of them that sleep. (1 Corinthians 15:20)

46. Chorus
Since by man came death, by man came also the resurrection of the dead.
For as in Adam all die, even so in Christ shall all be made alive. (1 Corinthians 15:21–22)

Introduction to Part III

Anyone listening to *Messiah* for the very first time might well imagine that the 'Hallelujah' Chorus is the last item in the whole work. After all, Parts I and II have covered the whole course of Jesus' ministry from Old Testament expectation to his coming to earth – and from his birth, via his ministry, sufferings, death, resurrection and ascension, not forgetting the worldwide advance of the gospel, to his final triumph over his enemies. The only significant element missing is Christ's second coming, as was discussed at the beginning of the last movement. On top of all that, Handel's superb musical offering in the 'Hallelujah' Chorus could hardly be surpassed.

Yet there is a third part to the oratorio, and it focuses on the themes of victory over death and of the future resurrection of Christian believers. The message of the Messiah's finished work, as spelt out in Parts I and II, is now applied in Part III to Christians of today, in order to give them confident hope and assurance in facing up to the reality of death. Death will not have the last word, for – in the apostle Paul's words – Jesus has 'abolished death and brought life and immortality to light through the gospel' (2 Tim 1:10). Musically, too, Part III does not disappoint, and there are some real gems of Handel's craftsmanship in the closing movements of the work.

A living Redeemer: Job 19:25–26

Movement 45 is the much-loved soprano air, *'I know that my Redeemer liveth',* based on the amazing words of Job in 19:25–26, where Job announces his belief in the certainty that beyond death he would enjoy full personal communion with God his redeemer and would do so in a new physical body replacing the one that has perished in the grave. Job's confident expectation for the future extends into verse 27 of the chapter, and for that reason it will be helpful to set out the three verses of Job's statement of faith as they appear in the ESV:

> For I know that my Redeemer lives,
> and that at the last he will stand upon the earth.
> And after my skin has been destroyed,
> yet in my flesh I shall see God,
> whom I shall see for myself,
> and my eyes shall behold, and not another.
> My heart faints within me! (Job 19:25–27)

There is every reason to believe that Handel felt personally involved in the writing of this movement, possibly to a greater extent than in the writing of any other, because of a bereavement within his own family. On 8 August 1718, Handel's sister, Dorothea Sophia, to whom he was much attached, died of tuberculosis at Halle. She was no older than 30. The sermon preached at her funeral has been preserved and it tells us that one of her favourite Bible verses, which she often quoted, was Job 19:25: *'I know that my Redeemer liveth'.* It seems very probable that Handel's decision to give this air to a female voice was largely connected with the memory of Dorothea. It is very fitting that the statue of Handel on the wall above his tomb in Westminster Abbey shows the musical score of this air directly in front of him.

Job is presented in the Bible book that bears his name as 'a blameless and upright man, who fears God and turns away from evil' (Job 1:8). When Satan suggests that Job only worships God because it brings him prosperity and that God does not realise how shallow Job's devotion is, God allows Job to go through extreme suffering in order to vindicate his own honour before a watching cosmos. Despite all that he goes through, Job never loses his faith in God, and one of the high-water points in the Book is Job's statement in the verses under discussion here, Job 19:25–27.

The sufferings of Job are suggestive of the sufferings of the Messiah, which feature so prominently in Part II of this oratorio. Like Christ, Job is an innocent sufferer – although in Job's case it is not that he is sinless, but rather that he does not deserve the suffering he undergoes. Like Christ, he experiences loneliness beyond imagination, as he is accused and despised by family and friends. The pain, the darkness and the sense of God-forsakenness that Job went through all anticipate the agony of the Lord Jesus, which he endured at a far deeper level. There is a parallel too between God's restoration of Job and God's vindication of the Messiah in the resurrection.

Job's confident hope of a future resurrection stands poles apart from the bleak despair of the materialist and the atheist. Bertrand Russell famously wrote, 'I believe that when I die I shall rot, and nothing of my ego will survive.'[1] Those words were written in a spirit of stiff-upper-lip stoicism. But the cloak of noble heroism cannot hide the bleakness and hopelessness of such an outlook.

When we look at Job's statement in Job 19, there are some uncertainties about the exact meaning of the Hebrew of verse 26, in particular whether Job is expecting to see God 'in my flesh' or 'without my flesh' (see the ESV footnote). However, this in no way detracts from the amazing certainties that Job affirms at this point.

First, Job expresses certainty that God is the living God and therefore, by implication, it makes sense to claim a personal relationship with him. He is *'my redeemer'* (my emphasis). Job is far removed from any inclination towards an atheistic response like that of Russell. Job has no doubt that *'at the latter day'* – at some point in the future – God himself will set foot on the world he has made. God has set a date when all will meet with him.

---

[1] B. A. W. Russell, *What I Believe* (London: Routledge Classics, 2004), 7.

Second, Job expresses certainty that God is his *'redeemer.'* The Hebrew word translated here is *go'el,* which we find in the Book of Ruth in connection with Boaz. This word often carries the idea of a kinsman, who – as with Boaz – intervenes in a situation of family need. But the word is also used in the Old Testament to refer to Yahweh as the covenant God, who promises to 'redeem' his people from their oppression. Exodus 6:6 may be quoted as one example of this: 'I am the Lord, and I will bring you out from under the burdens of the Egyptians, and I will deliver you from slavery to them, and I will redeem you with an outstretched arm and with great acts of judgement.' Although God appears to be acting as his adversary, Job holds on to his belief that God will intervene personally on his behalf.

Third, Job expresses certainty about the future. Death does not bring annihilation but a transformed relationship with the living God. If the correct translation of verse 26 is *'in my flesh',* we have here a clear expression of Old Testament belief in physical resurrection, as in Daniel 12:2. But whether the correct reading is *'in my flesh'* or 'without my flesh', the threefold mention of the faculty of sight indicates a belief in some form of renewed physical ability: 'Yet in my flesh *I shall see* God, whom *I shall see* for myself, and *my eyes shall behold,* and not another' (v 26–27, ESV, my italics).

The risen Christ (1 Corinthians 15:20)

The content of Job's confidence about God and about the future is breathtaking. It is nothing less than an anticipation of the certainties that are expressed in clearer terms in the New Testament in the light of Jesus' own resurrection. Charles Jennens evidently recognised this, because so appropriately he concludes the soprano air of Movement 45 with 1 Corinthians 15:20: *'For now is Christ risen from the dead, the firstfruits of them that sleep.'*[2]

The fact that Jesus' rising again represents the *'firstfruits of them that sleep'* implies the certainty of later fruits. Jesus' resurrection is the

[2] Jennens has slightly changed the AV wording of this verse: '*But* now is Christ risen from the dead, *and become* the firstfruits of them that *slept*' (the three parts of the verse that have been amended are shown in italics).

guarantee of the future resurrection of all Christian believers. So certain is this prospect that death for the Christian is no longer something to be feared. That is the reason why Paul uses the word *'sleep'* instead of the word 'die.' In so doing, he follows the lead of the Lord Jesus himself, when he raised Jairus's daughter to life. Jesus said of her, 'The child is not dead but sleeping' (Mark 5:39). He was not denying that the girl had died, but was announcing that she would not remain dead. Her death was not final, as he demonstrated by raising her to life again. The Bible does not teach that Christians who die will sleep (or remain unconscious) until the Last Day. We have already noted Jesus' words of assurance to the penitent criminal who was crucified with him: 'Truly, I say to you, today you will be with me in Paradise' (Luke 23:43). So the assurance for Christian believers today from the raising of Jairus's daughter from the dead (and reinforced by the word 'sleep' in 1 Corinthians 15:20) is that, when a Christian dies, it is as if they fall asleep in order to wake up immediately in the presence of Jesus.

The resurrection of Jesus transforms everything and for ever. In the words of C S Lewis:

> He (Christ) has forced open a door that has been locked since the death of the first man. He has met, fought and beaten the King of Death. Everything is different because he has done so. This is the beginning of the new creation: a new chapter in cosmic history has opened.[3]

Death in Adam but life in Christ (1 Corinthians 15:21–22)

Jennens remains in 1 Corinthians 15 for the next movement, using the next two verses – verses 21 and 22. The following two scenes will use verses from the later part of that chapter. 1 Corinthians 15 is undeniably the chapter *par excellence* on the subject of resurrection: both Jesus' own bodily resurrection and the future bodily resurrection of Christian believers. A reading of the whole chapter is to be recommended.

[3] Lewis, *Miracles*, 149.

Movement 46, the chorus *'Since by man came death',* takes us to the very next two verses of 1 Corinthians 15, verses 21 and 22, where Paul sets out a twofold contrast between Adam and Christ, who is described as a second Adam:

> For as by a man came death,
> by a man has come also the resurrection of the dead.
> For as in Adam all die,
> so also in Christ shall all be made alive.
> (1 Cor 15:21–22)

A helpful picture of the contrast between Adam and Christ is provided by the Puritan pastor Thomas Goodwin. In an exposition entitled 'Christ set forth' he imagines Adam and Christ as two great giants, each wearing an enormous belt with millions of little hooks on it.[4] All mankind are hanging either at Adam's or at Christ's belt. In passing, we may note the Bible's testimony to the historicity of Adam, as the contrast between Adam and Christ makes sense only if both are real individuals. Paul develops the contrast between Adam and Christ, and the two humanities who find in each their federal head, more fully in Romans 5:12–21. Here in 1 Corinthians 15:21–22 the contrasts are set out much more concisely.

'By a man came death' (1 Cor 15:21) points us to the Fall in Genesis 3. God had announced to Adam and Eve what would happen if they ate of the tree of the knowledge of good and evil. He said, 'for in the day that you eat of it you shall surely die' (Gen 2:17). To eat the fruit of this tree would be to express independence of God. It would be to set themselves up as God and to decide for themselves what is good and evil, rather than living under his rule and faithfully obeying his commands. Their disobedience resulted in 'death', just as God said it would. In the first place, death was experienced *physically*, because that would now be the normal pattern for every member of the human race. Although Adam and Eve remained alive for many years to come, the process of physical decay in their mortal bodies set in from that time onwards. In the second place, death was experienced *spiritually* then and there in the Garden in Genesis 3, because Adam and Eve lost their intimate fellowship with God and were

---

[4] See G.J. Williams, *His Love Endures For Ever* (Nottingham: Inter-Varsity Press, 2015), 177.

ejected from the Garden, in the middle of which the tree of life was to be found (Gen 2:9), and from God's presence (Gen 3:22–24).

'For as in Adam all die' (1 Cor 15:22) spells out the experience of mankind from that fateful day onwards. It speaks of our essential solidarity with Adam, which is a solidarity of guilt, because the human race is one single entity. Because of Adam, each of us is born as a sinner. This is what David meant when he wrote, 'Behold, I was brought forth in iniquity, and in sin did my mother conceive me' (Ps 51:5). Before ever I committed a sin, I was a sinner, so that the problem about my relationship with God is not simply my 'sins', but the underlying 'sin' with which I was born. In medical terms, the symptoms of the disease of the human race are 'sins', but the condition of the patient is 'sin.' What makes the situation so serious is that the sin-disease is terminal: untreated, it leads to death for every single human being – both *physically* (the fact that one or two individuals have been taken to God without passing through death – Enoch, Gen 5:24, and Elijah, 2 Kings 2:11 – only underlines the rule to which they are the exception) and *spiritually* (what the Book of Revelation calls 'the second death', Rev 2:11, 20:6, 21:8).

Following the account, in these last two paragraphs, of the bad news, we turn now with relief to the good news which is presented to us in 1 Corinthians 15:21b and 15:22b. Just as death came into the world through Adam, so life came into the world through Christ. 'By a man' in the second half of verse 21 underlines the reality of the incarnation. Christ had to be as truly a man as was Adam. If death entered the human race 'by a man', so also 'by a man' it had to be overcome.

In verse 22, we are told that just as Adam's sin brought untold consequences of evil, so Christ's work brought untold consequences of good: 'so also in Christ shall all be made alive' encompasses more than resurrection (wonderful as that is) It includes also the thought of the abundant life that Jesus promises to all who are in him (John 10:10). But the 'all' in the two halves of verse 22 are not identical. The 'all' who are 'in Adam' are all mankind as they are born into this world until, and unless, they are transferred from being 'in Adam' to being 'in Christ.' The 'all', therefore, who are 'in Christ' are all Christians: those who by receiving Jesus and believing in his name have been given 'the right to become the children of God' (John 1:12), those who by God's Spirit have been 'born again' (John 3:7–8), those whom God 'has delivered ... from the domain of darkness and transferred ... to the kingdom of his beloved Son' (Col 1:13).

There is no place here for universalism – in other words, the idea that all people will automatically go to heaven. Every individual person lives as a member of one or other of the two humanities, whose heads are the old Adam and the new Adam (Christ). The grace of the gospel means that it is possible for 'whoever believes in him' to pass from death to life, from perishing to eternal life (John 3:16, 5:24). In this connection, it might be helpful to return to Thomas Goodwin's picture of Adam and Christ as two giants with their belts: 'these two between them', he writes, 'had all the rest of the sons of men hanging at their girdle.'[5] The offer of the Christian gospel is that people can, by God's grace, be unhooked from Adam's belt and hooked on to Christ's, so that they have a different head, an adequate mediator, a new representative.

---

[5] Cited in Williams, *His Love Endures For Ever*, 177.

What to listen out for in the music in Part III Scene 1

45. Air: *'I know that my redeemer liveth'*

The music of this movement contrasts in many ways with the preceding 'Hallelujah' Chorus. Instead of a mainly *forte* chorus with trumpets and timpani, we have a gentle, quieter solo air. If the 'Hallelujah' Chorus conveys exuberant praise, this piece breathes a spirit of confident simplicity.

The soloist's certainty is emphasised by the E major melody's initial upward leap to a strong beat on the word *'know'*, a feature which recurs in nearly all the uses of the phrase *'I know.'* This is another important occurrence of the ascending fourth, which has been commented on as the unifying motif of the oratorio.

Very near the end of the movement the words *'for now is Christ risen'* are set to an ascending melody of just over an octave. This may be regarded as another example of musical onomatopoeia: the 'rising' expressed in the words is depicted by the 'rising' shape of the melodic line.

46. Chorus: *'Since by man came death'*

Musically, this chorus is brief – a mere 37 bars – but the way in which it conveys the contrast within each of the two verses, which has been discussed above, is masterful. Not surprisingly, given that we have here two verses of Scripture, each of which sets out its contrast between Adam and Christ in two halves, the chorus is made up of four parts: one for each half-verse.

The first and third parts, focusing on Adam and death, are marked *piano* and *grave* – they are both unaccompanied (the technical term is *a cappella*), which focuses attention all the more on the seriousness of the words.

By contrast, the second and fourth quarters, which speak of Christ and resurrection, are brisk (the marking is *allegro* and *forte.*)

Block chord style is used throughout, and the music engages the listener's attention by some striking chromatic chord progressions, particularly in the first and third quarters.

Part III Scene 2: The Messiah's Victory Means the Resurrection of the Body – 2

47. *Accompagnato* (bass)
    Behold, I tell you a mystery; we shall not all sleep, but we shall all be changed, in a moment, in the twinkling of an eye, at the last trumpet. (1 Corinthians 15:51–52)
48. Air (bass)
    The trumpet shall sound, and the dead shall be raised incorruptible, and we shall be changed.
    For this corruptible must put on incorruption, and this mortal must put on immortality. (1 Corinthians 15:52–53)

The future resurrection of Christian believers (1 Corinthians 15:51–53)

Movement 47 is a bass *accompagnato*, using verses 51–52a of the chapter. *'Behold'* (literally, 'Look!') calls for the attention of the reader or listener. *'I tell you a mystery'*, the verse continues. *'Mystery'* (or 'secret') does not mean a puzzle which we find difficult to solve, but a secret which by ourselves we are wholly unable to penetrate, but which God has now revealed. So *'mystery'* in the Bible indicates an open secret. It is open only because God has graciously made it known, and never could we by ourselves have worked out the truth of the future resurrection of Christian believers.

'We shall not all sleep, but we shall all be changed.' As we saw above, in the discussion of 1 Corinthians 15:20, to *'sleep'* means to 'die'. Despite what some people have claimed about Paul, he never taught that the second coming would definitely take place in his lifetime. Rather, he knew that at some point in time there will be a generation of Christian believers who will not die or sleep, because Christ will return while they are about their normal activities. So the first *'we'* in this verse is pointing to Christian believers who are alive on that day.

But for all Christian believers, regardless of whether they have died before that great day or are still alive, *'we shall all be changed'*. The Bible tells us that there will be a resurrection for all mankind, both Christians and non-Christians (Dan 12:2, Matt 25:46, John 5:28–29, Acts 24:15, Rev 20:12–13): the 'resurrection of life' and 'the resurrection of judgement'. But in 1 Corinthians 15 Paul is writing about the resurrection of Christian believers.

The change will be instantaneous. *'In a moment'* translates the word from which we derive our English word 'atom', meaning 'that which cannot be divided', the smallest amount of time possible. The phrase *'in the twinkling of an eye'*, meaning the time it takes to cast a glance, has been in use since 1302 and is to be found in all major Bible translations, including William Tyndale's New Testament and the AV.

'The last trumpet' is linked in Jesus' teaching with the events of the end of time (Matt 24:31) and Paul refers to it in 1 Thessalonians 4:16 in connection with Christ's return: it is the signal for the dead to rise.

Movement 48 is a bass air, which continues with the second half of 1 Corinthians 15:52 and takes us also into verse 53. These verses focus on the great transformation which will take place on the day of Christ's return, when *'the trumpet shall sound, and the dead shall be raised incorruptible.'* The last word is rendered 'imperishable' in the ESV.

Then, at the end of verse 52, Paul repeats his statement that *'we shall be changed'*. The new order of existence will be radically different. In verse 53, Paul expands on this great change and highlights in particular the ending of all that is *'corruptible'* (in other words, 'perishable') and *'mortal'*. Decay and death will be no more.

So, in one sense, there will be a real discontinuity between what the old and the new. But there is a real continuity too, which was hinted at above, and this is made clearer in the next two verses (v 53–54a) by the fourfold use of the word *'this'*, which is found in the AV – two in verse 53 and two in verse 54. Modern translations make this difficult to spot: the NIV omits all four instances of the word *'this'*, and the ESV retains only the first two.

We meet just the first two occurrences of the word *'this'* in Movement 48, as Charles Jennens edits out the first half of verse 54. He continues with the second half of verse 54 in the next movement. Here, then is yet another instance of a half-verse being omitted from the libretto. We might surmise that Jennens felt that the substance of the first half of verse 54 repeats essentially the content of verse 53.

The thought that 'this perishable body must put on the imperishable' (v 53, ESV), and the repeated use of the phrase *'put on'* (as if these things were items of clothing) indicate that the body is not the real person but an outer layer. It is as if, in the life to come, the real person will put on another suit of clothes.

What to listen out for in the music in Part III Scene 2

47. *Accompagnato: 'Behold, I tell you a mystery'*

This short bass *accompagnato* acts as an introduction to the next movement not only through the sequence of Bible verses but also musically in two ways. The key is D major, which is also that of the following air, and motifs like trumpet signals appear in the strings even before the last words *'at the last trumpet.'*

48. Air: *'The trumpet shall sound'*

Musically, this movement is always very popular, not least because of the exciting trumpet *obbligato* that is used throughout the air, representing *'the last trumpet'* (the word *obbligato* is the technical word for an instrumental part that is essential to the effect desired).

Not surprisingly, as with the earlier movements which included the trumpets ('Glory to God' and the 'Hallelujah' Chorus), the key is D major, which showcases the trumpet to its best advantage.

The air is set in ternary form (otherwise known as a *da capo* air). The A-section of the beginning and end is made up of the words of verse 53, and the central B-section is made up of the words of verse 54a.

In *'and we shall be changed'* the word *'changed'* is treated in inventive ever-changing *melismas* of up to six bars (as noted on earlier occasions, a *melisma* is when one syllable flowers out into a passage of several notes).

In the middle section the word *'immortality'* is expressed in lively *melismas* of even greater numbers of bars.

Part III Scene 3: The Messiah's Victory Means the Defeat of Death and Sin

49. **Recitative (contralto)**
    Then shall be brought to pass the saying that is written, Death is swallowed up in victory. (1 Corinthians 15:54b)
50. **Duet (contralto and tenor)**
    O death, where is thy sting? O grave, where is thy victory? The sting of death is sin, and the strength of sin is the law. (1 Corinthians 15:55–56)
51. **Chorus**
    But thanks be to God, who giveth us the victory through our Lord Jesus Christ. (1 Corinthians 15:57)
52. **Air (soprano)**
    If God is for us, who can be against us? Who shall lay anything to the charge of God's elect?
    It is God that justifieth. Who is he that condemneth? It is Christ that died, yea rather, that is risen again, who is at the right hand of God, who makes intercession for us. (Romans 8:31b, 33–34)

The death of death (1 Corinthians 15:54–57)

The first three movements of this scene continue to take us through the closing section of 1 Corinthians 15, although Jennens omits the first half of verse 54. He also omits the final verse of the chapter, verse 58, which represents the practical application of the whole chapter.[1]

Movement 49 is a contralto recitative announcing that, on that last day when Christ returns, the Old Testament prophecy concerning the complete victory over death will be fulfilled. The Old Testament verse quoted is from Isaiah 25:8, which reads as follows in full:

---

[1] 1 Corinthians 15:58 reads: 'Therefore, my beloved brothers, be steadfast, immovable, always abounding in the work of the Lord, knowing that in the Lord your labour is not in vain.'

> He will swallow up death for ever;
> and the Lord God will wipe away tears from all faces,
> and the reproach of his people he will take away from all the earth,
> for the Lord has spoken.

'Swallowed up in victory' is a powerful metaphor for the complete destruction of death. The reference to God wiping away tears from all faces is echoed in Revelation 21:4 as part of the picture of the new heaven and the new earth, where there will be unbroken fellowship between God and his people. 'Reproach' is a reminder of the curse that death, as the consequence of sin, represents for the human race, but one day it will be completely removed.

Movement 50 is a setting of the next two verses in 1 Corinthians 15, verses 55–56, which explore two themes: another Old Testament anticipation of the victory over death, this time from Hosea 13:14; and an explanation of the relationship between death, sin and the law.

The tone of verse 55 is exultation. This is a victory cry over a defeated enemy. The fact that we will still have to face death (unless we belong to that generation who are still alive at Christ's second coming) does not lessen the certainty or the joy. The picture in the first half of the verse is of a bee or a scorpion, whose harmful sting Christ has drawn by taking it upon himself, and therefore death is now harmless to all who are in him. Verse 56 goes on to explain that it is not death itself that is harmful, but the fact that death is 'the wages of sin' (Rom 6:23). The *'sting'* of death is *'sin.'* But now that sin is pardoned, as far as the Christian believer is concerned, death has no sting – Christ has paid the price for sin once and for all. This is the glorious truth for Christian believers, but the assurances of these verses do not apply to those whose sin remains unforgiven.

Sin has an unexpected ally, from which it derives its power, namely *'the law.'* The law is of divine origin and is therefore 'holy and righteous and good' (Rom 7:12), but the law is totally incapable of offering salvation (see Rom 5:12ff, 7:7ff, 10:4). The law sets the standard we ought to reach but never do. The law takes us prisoner and condemns us.

The Christian believer can look back on that predicament and thank Christ for deliverance – which is exactly what happens in verse 57 (the subject matter of Movement 51, a chorus). *'Through our Lord Jesus Christ'* we (in other words, Christian believers) have been given *'the victory'* over death and sin and law. The victory in each of those three domains needs to be spelt out:

- Christ is victorious over *death:* 'We know that Christ being raised from the dead will never die again; death no longer has dominion over him' (Rom 6:9).
- He has satisfied the *law*'s demands, for 'Christ redeemed us from the curse of the law by becoming a curse for us' (Gal 3:13).
- He has replaced the 'reign' of *sin* with that of grace (Rom 5:20–21).

While this victory, in its completeness, still belongs to the future, the thought here is that Christian believers share in that victory now on a daily basis, as a result of all that Christ has done on our behalf. While this victory, in its completeness, still belongs to the future, the thought here is that Christian believers share in that victory now on a daily basis, as a result of all that Christ has done on our behalf. It is important for Christian believers to maintain the right balance between the "now" and the "not yet." On the one hand, we are to lay hold in assurance of all that God has made available to us here and now in this life (e.g. forgiveness and assurance of Christ's indwelling presence by his Spirit). On the other hand, we should be content to look forward to blessings which will be ours only in heaven (e.g. sinlessness and redemption of the body). So, in connection with the 'victory', promised in 1 Corinthians 15:57, it is true, on the one hand, that we have it now, because God 'gives' it to us. Bishop Taylor Smith once commented, with defeatist believers in mind, 'It is not for us to obtain the victory, but to appropriate the victory Christ has obtained.'[2] On the other hand, we need to recognise that we look forward to far more in heaven than we can ever experience on earth.

---

[2] E. L. Langston, *Great Churchmen: John Taylor Smith* (Vol. 15) (Cited from the Church Society website: http://churchsociety.org/resources/page/great_churchmen).

Jesus' victory is the only answer to death

Death is surely the great taboo subject of the early twenty-first century and has been for some time. It is the subject that people so often wish to avoid. We should not be surprised that the non-Christian world should shy away from the subject of death, as it has no answers at all. This sombre reality is acknowledged by pagans of the past and the present. As typical of pagans of the ancient world we can take Aristotle's comment: 'Death is a dreadful thing, for it is the end.'[3] Among more modern-day pagans, we have already quoted Bertrand Russell's view about what happens at death. In similar vein, when Thomas Huxley's mother died, all he could write to his sister was: 'My dearest sister, I offer you no consolation, for I know of none. There are things which each must bear as best he may with the strength that has been allotted to him.'[4]

One significant feature of modern society is the way it often adopts a sentimental or escapist view of death. A popular choice of reading at crematoriums is the piece by Henry Scott Holland, which begins, 'Death is nothing at all ... I have only slipped away in to the next room'.[5] But that is simply not true. The problem about death is that it is not 'nothing', and the separation it brings about is far wider than the wall between two rooms.

If it was not this particular piece, it was certainly this type of approach that C S Lewis had in mind when, in his book *Pilgrim's Regress*, the main character encounters Death, who speaks these words:

> Do not think that you can escape me; do not think that you can call me Nothing. To you I am not Nothing; I am the being blindfolded, the losing all power of self-defence, the surrender, not because any terms are offered, but because resistance is gone: the step into the dark: the defeat of all precautions: utter

---

[3] Cited in J. Blanchard, *Right with God* (Edinburgh: The Banner of Trust, 1985), 78.

[4] Cited in L. Huxley, *Life and Letters of Thomas Henry Huxley* (Cambridge: Cambridge University Press, 1903), volume 1, 144.

[5] Henry Scott Holland, *Death is Nothing at All* (London: Souvenir Press Ltd, 1987).

> hopelessness turned out to utter risk: the final loss of liberty. The Landlord's Son who feared nothing feared me.[6]

'The Landlord's Son' refers, of course, to Jesus.[7] No doubt, what C S Lewis had in mind here were incidents in the Gospels when we read of Jesus, mindful of his coming 'hour' (in other words, the cross), saying, 'Now is my soul troubled' (John 12:27), or of the description of him in the Garden of Gethsemane as 'greatly distressed and troubled' and saying, 'My soul is very sorrowful, even to death' (Mark 14:33–34). But there was a particular reason why Jesus experienced this distress and anguish as he faced his coming crucifixion. In a unique way, Jesus was preparing to face not just physical death but the full 'sting' of death, to refer again to 1 Corinthians 15:56. What lay before him can only be termed as spiritual death. On the cross he suffered separation from the Father, as he bore our guilt and penalty, and experienced the terrors of hell (as was discussed earlier on in connection with Scenes 1 and 2 of Part II of the oratorio).

The glorious outcome of Jesus' ordeal on our behalf is, of course, that those who follow after him and look to him need never fear death. Latimer and Ridley, whom we met in an earlier discussion, and countless other Christians all down the ages, have been able to face death with courage and composure. They were able to do this <u>because</u> Jesus met the real Death in single combat on the Cross. In so doing he stripped Death of its terrors and drew its *"sting"* by virtue of his substitutionary sacrifice and his own sinless obedience.

It is important to understand that the only answer to death is to be found in Christ's victory, won on the cross. Paul writes of Jesus' death at Calvary that God 'disarmed the rulers and authorities and put them to open shame, by triumphing over them in him' (Col 2:15).[8] Another important passage about the victory over death, achieved by the cross, is Hebrews 2:14–15:

---

[6] C. S. Lewis, *The Pilgrim's Regress* (Glasgow: Collins/Fount, 1977), 212.

[7] This title for Jesus is drawn from Christ's own Parable of the Tenants (Mark 12:1-11), in which he foretells his imminent death. In the AV the owner of the vineyard, representing God, is described as the 'lord' of the vineyard (v 9).

[8] 'In him' means 'in Jesus' – or, following the ESV footnote, 'in it', in other words, the cross.

> Since therefore the children share in flesh and blood, he himself likewise partook of the same things, that through death he might destroy the one who has the power of death, that is, the devil, and deliver all those who through fear of death were subject to lifelong slavery.

In both these New Testament quotations (Col.2:15 and Heb.2:14-15) we are told that the victory won is not only over sin and death, but over the spiritual powers behind them, in particular Satan. The Gospels show us that Jesus came "to destroy the works of the devil" (1 Jn.3.9). We see therefore that, although Satan is "a strong man" who guards his palace and keeps his goods safe, Jesus is "one stronger than he." He (Jesus) "attacks him and overcomes him, he takes away his armour in which he trusted and divides his spoil" (Lk.11:21-22).

In 1 Corinthians 15:26, the apostle Paul tells us, 'The last enemy to be destroyed is death.' As we have already seen, Easter Day is the public demonstration of the reality of the victory that was won on Good Friday. On Good Friday, death died; on Easter Day, the death announcement was made public. The cross and the resurrection, which belong inseparably together, assure us of Christ's supremacy. In the words of the hymn 'Guide Me, O Thou Great Jehovah', he himself is 'death of death and hell's destruction'.[9] What magnificent titles for our Saviour and Lord! Now we can look forward to the day when the fruits of that victory will be enjoyed in full measure.

This section concludes with two great statements of the assurance that all Christian believers can have in the face of death. The first is from John Donne:

> Death, be not proud, though some have called thee
> Mighty and dreadful, for thou art not so;
> For those whom thou think'st thou dost overthrow
> Die not, poor Death, nor yet canst thou kill me ...

---

[9] *Guide me, O Thou Great Jehovah,* also found as *Guide me, O my Great Redeemer.* Text by William Williams (1745) – translated from Welsh into English by Peter Williams (1771).

One short sleep past, we wake eternally
And death shall be no more; Death, thou shalt die.[10]

The other is from Martin Luther:

> When I feel the dread of death, I say, 'O death, you have nothing to do with me, because I have another death which kills my death. And the death which kills is stronger than that which is killed.'[11]

The full assurance of Christian believers (Romans 8:31–34)

Movement 52, which is an air, is a setting of Romans 8:31b, 33 and 34. As a contrast to the following choral conclusion of the oratorio, it is sung by the soprano soloist.

We have seen that Charles Jennens chooses not to include the final verse of 1 Corinthians 15 (verse 58), even though he has made use of the rest of the concluding section of the chapter from verse 51 onwards. That final verse of the chapter would have supplied Paul's own practical exhortation to live a life of Christian stability in the light of the truths of resurrection. Instead, Jennens has decided to round off this scene with a different exhortation from the Apostle Paul and has selected a few verses from towards the end of another great Bible chapter, Romans chapter 8.

Why has Jennens made this choice? My personal view is that he had two considerations in mind:

First, he may well have wished to continue the theme of assurance that runs through Part III, from the very first item (*'I know that my Redeemer liveth'*, my emphasis) onwards. He may possibly have felt that 1 Corinthians 15:58 did not sound the note of the Christian's assured standing before God as clearly as he wished.

Secondly, he may well have been drawn to Romans 8:34 with its focus on *'Christ ... who is at the right hand of God'* as a preparation for the

[10] A. Quiller-Couch (ed.), *The Oxford Book of English Verse 1250-1918* (Oxford: Oxford University Press, 1939), 238.
[11] Cited in Atkinson, *The Darkness of Faith: Daily Readings with Martin Luther,* 52.

following movement with its vision of all praise and glory being ascribed to *'him that sitteth upon the throne and unto the Lamb.'*

Romans 8 combines the two themes of the inevitability of suffering and 'groaning' here and now and of the certainty of glory and full salvation in heaven to come. In the closing section of the chapter, Paul asks five questions in order to heighten his readers' awareness of the immensity of God's everlasting love.

Here are the five questions as they appear in the ESV, following an introductory question in the first half of verse 31 ('What then shall we say to these things?'), from halfway through verse 31 to verse 35, together with an occasional additional comment from the apostle. The parts that Jennens uses are in bold:

- **If God is for us, who can be against us?** (v 31b)
- He who did not spare his own Son but gave him up for us all, how will he not also with him graciously give us all things? (v 32)
- **Who shall bring any charge against God's elect? It is God who justifies.** (v 33)
- **Who is to condemn? Christ Jesus is the one who died – more than that, who was raised – who is at the right hand of God, who indeed is interceding for us.** (v 34)
- Who shall separate us from the love of Christ? (v 35a)

This last question is stated again in a different way in verse 35b.

Each time there can be no answer to the question, or the implied answer is 'Nobody!' or 'Nothing!' In this way Paul shows how immeasurably great is God's sovereign grace.

'If God is for us, who can be against us?' (v 31b). Despite any amount of opposition, victory is secure, because even one man or woman with the Lord God constitutes a majority.

John Wesley referred to Romans 8:31 in a letter to William Wilberforce, in order to encourage him at a time when he experienced opposition in his long campaign to abolish the slave trade:

> Unless God has raised you up for this very thing, you will be worn out by the opposition of men and devils. But if God be for you, who can be against you? Are all of them stronger than God?'[12]

'Who shall lay anything to the charge of God's elect? It is God that justifieth. Who is he that condemneth? It is Christ that died, yea rather, that is risen again, who is at the right hand of God, who makes intercession for us' (v 33–34). As we have already seen, the devil is an accuser (Job 1–2; also in Rev 12:10), but Christ has dealt with all our sins, and his risen presence at the Father's right hand is the guarantee that the price has been paid. On top of that, we are assured that he himself prays for us, on the basis of his own finished work, to make our acceptance before God even more secure.

We may wish that Jennens had included some at least of verses 35–39 of Romans 8, from which so many Christian believers throughout the centuries have derived great assurance.

As an example of one such instance, here is the record of the final moments of Robert Bruce, a seventeenth century Scottish minister. He was sitting at breakfast with his family, when he realised that he was dying. He called for his family Bible, but finding that he could not see, he said,

> Cast up to me the eighth chapter of the epistle to the Romans, and set my finger on these words, 'I am persuaded that neither death, nor life, nor angels, nor principalities, nor powers, nor things present, nor things to come, nor height, nor depth, nor any other creature, shall be able to separate us from the love of God which is in Christ Jesus our Lord.' Now, is my finger upon them?[13]

---

[12] This was Wesley's very last letter, written on his deathbed on 24 February 1791, six days before his death – see http://www.christianitytoday.com/history/issues/issue-2/wesley-to-wilberforce.html.

[13] H. Lockyer, *Last Words of Saints and Sinners* (Grand Rapids: Kregel Publications, 1969), 187. The Bible quotation is Romans 8:38-39.

Being it told it was, he said, 'God be with you, my children. I have breakfasted with you, and shall sup with my Lord Jesus Christ this night.' Then with his hand on the page of Romans 8, he said, 'I die, believing these words.'[14]

As already pointed out, Charles Jennens has made use of only a small part of the closing section of Romans 8, touching only on the above-mentioned areas of adversaries and accusations. This may be a matter of disappointment for some. But we have to recognise, once again, Jennens's need to make editorial cuts.

It is to be hoped that the Bible verses that are included in the libretto will point the listener to their place within their larger context.

What to listen out for in the music in Part III Scene 3

49. Recitative: *'Then shall be brought to pass'*

A short recitative.

50. Duet: *'O death, where is thy sting?'*

Movement 50 is a duet – the only genuine duet in the oratorio – for contralto and tenor. In the other item marked 'Duet', Movement 20, the two voices sing the two parts of the piece separately.

51. Chorus: *'But thanks be to God'*

The chorus answers the question of the preceding movement in the same key and tempo.

52. Air: *'If God is for us, who can be against us?'*

As a contrast to the following choral conclusion of the oratorio, this movement is sung by the soprano soloist. This is, of course, a very simple device on Handel's part, but highly effective, as the following movement comes over to the audience with heightened impact.

[14] Lockyer, *Last Words of Saints and Sinners.*

Part III Scene 4: The Messiah is worthy of all honour

53. Chorus

Worthy is the Lamb that was slain, and hath redeemed us to God by his blood, to receive power, and riches, and wisdom, and strength, and honour, and glory, and blessing.
Blessing and honour, glory and power be unto him that sitteth upon the throne, and unto the Lamb, for ever and ever. Amen. (Revelation 5:12–14, plus part of v9)

Worthy is the Lamb

Movement 53 falls into two parts. First, there is a chorus with the words taken from Revelation 5:12–13, *'Worthy is the Lamb'*, together with a phrase transferred from verse 9. Secondly, to round off the oratorio, is another chorus, the celebrated 'Amen Chorus', which uses the single word *'Amen'* from the following verse, Revelation 5:14.

Where else could Charles Jennens take us in this closing movement of the whole work than where he has already taken us at the end of Part II in the 'Hallelujah' Chorus – namely once again into heaven itself? Here we have the song of praise around the throne of God, voiced by 'many angels, numbering myriads of myriads and thousands of thousands' (Rev 5:11), followed by every being in the whole of creation ascribing eternal 'blessing and honour and glory and might' to the Father and the Son (Rev 5:12).

The Book of Revelation opens with the apostle John's vision of the glorified Christ (Rev 1) and Christ's letters to the seven churches (Rev 2–3). Then, in chapters 4 and 5 (which make up a single unit), John is given a vision of the throne room of heaven. Chapter 4 presents a picture of the almost indescribable glory of God, surrounded by the awesome four living creatures and the twenty-four elders, who praise God in particular as Creator:

> Worthy are you, our Lord and God,
> to receive glory and honour and power,
> for you created all things,
> and by your will they existed and were created.
> (Rev 4:11)

Chapter 5 takes us from the theme of creation to that of salvation. Our attention is drawn to a sealed scroll held in the hand of God. As the Book of Revelation will make plain in later chapters, that scroll contains God's judgement on the world, where – in contrast to the inhabitants of heaven – men and women by and large do not honour God. The scroll also contains and God's rescue of his people. But who will break the seals and open the scroll? Who is worthy of such a role? The implication is that only someone with divine authority to execute God's judgement and with the quality of life to provide salvation is qualified.

At first no one is found. But then John's attention is directed to 'the Lion of Judah, the root of David', the one who has 'conquered' and is therefore able to open the sealed scroll (v 5). The first of those titles comes from Genesis 49:9 and the second from Isaiah 11:1: They refer to the Messiah, the one with all authority and royal power.

Immediately there is a surprise in the narrative of Revelation 5 because, when John turns to look at this Messianic figure, he sees 'a Lamb standing, as though it had been slain' (v 6). The Lion and the Lamb are one and the same individual. Christ the Lion has conquered and overcome by being slaughtered like a Lamb.

This combination of roles in the person of the Messiah comes as no surprise to those who have worked their way through the content of the oratorio, because Charles Jennens has spelt out this stupendous truth for us in his judicious selection of Bible material. The whole of the oratorio prepares us for this Bible verse which merges together the kingly rule and the sacrificial death of Christ. So, for example, we have seen that Jesus is the Messianic King of Psalm 2 (Movements 40–43) and that he is 'the Lamb of God who takes away the sin of the world' (Movements 22–30). He is the one who alone is qualified to exercise both judgement and salvation with justice and mercy.

A further reference to the writings of C S Lewis is relevant here. He clearly has this dual identity of Christ in mind in the closing pages of *The Voyage of the Dawn Treader*, when the children meet a lamb who changes into the lion, Aslan. What is particularly significant in this episode for readers of the Narnia chronicles is that this is one of the most explicit identifications of Aslan as Christ in the whole series of books, enhanced by deliberate echoes of the disciples' breakfast meeting with the Risen Christ in John 21.[1]

In Revelation 5, as the Lamb takes the scroll from God's right hand, the four living creatures and the 24 elders sing 'a new song':

> Worthy are you to take the scroll and to open its seals,
> for you were slain, and by your blood you ransomed
> people for God
> from every tribe and language and people and nation,
> and you have made them a kingdom and priests to our
> God, and they shall reign on earth (Rev 5:9–10).

This song is a parallel to the previous one in 4:11, which was ascribed to God the Father. As has been indicated already, the praise of chapter 4 focuses on creation, while this one in chapter 5 focuses on redemption and salvation.

We notice the scope of the achievement of the Lord Jesus Christ: it is truly multinational – which should sound an echo of Acts 2, when the Holy Spirit empowered the first Christian disciples to proclaim the gospel to a multinational audience. One of the functions of the Day of Pentecost, therefore, was to provide an anticipation of heaven to come.

We notice too, in Revelation 5, the fruit of Christ's finished work in two ways. First, all his people are 'priests': here is the priesthood of all believers, in the sense of their being entrusted with the task of holding out to men and women the gospel, by which they can be reconciled to God. Second, Christians 'reign' on earth with the dignity of being sons and daughters of the living God.

The text of this great chorus in the oratorio picks up from the beginning of verse 12, with the countless multitude of heaven declaring words praising Christ for his role as the atoning sacrifice which has won his people's redemption: '*Worthy is the Lamb that was slain*'.

---

[1] Lewis, *The Voyage of the Dawn Treader,* 208–9.

At this point in the text Jennens inserts a phrase which he has lifted from verse 9, in order to amplify and reinforce the Lamb's great achievement by his death on the cross: *'and hath redeemed us to God by his blood'*. We have noticed elsewhere how Jennens has omitted an occasional verse or half-verse without the listener necessarily being aware of it. Here, however, he adds part of a verse – similarly without the listener necessarily being aware. And it has to be added that he does it not only seamlessly but also effectively.

At the end of verse 12, seven expressions are used to describe the splendour of the Lamb. In the Book of Revelation, the number seven is regularly used to indicate completeness (as was noted in the earlier discussion of the verses from Revelation used in the 'Hallelujah' Chorus), and there is little doubt that that is what is intended here. The first four expressions spell out qualities which he has in his own right (*'power, and riches, and wisdom, and strength'*), and the other three express his people's attitude to him (*'honour, and glory, and blessing'*). As the whole of creation takes up the angels' praise in verse 13, four qualities are specified (*'blessing and honour, glory and power'*).

Significant also is the way Revelation 5:13 links *'him that sitteth upon the throne'* and *'the Lamb'* in a way that shows unmistakably that the Lamb is enthroned with God as God. We have here a pictorial representation of the second and third phrase of John 1:1 (where, of course, Jesus is described as 'the Word' rather than 'the Lamb'): 'and the Word was with God, and the Word was God.'

The second part of Movement 53 concentrates on the single word *'Amen!'* which is uttered in the following verse by the four living creatures in response to the song of praise of verses 12 and 13. 'Amen' means 'So be it.' What else is there to say? The word is sung repeatedly, but not repetitiously, and allows the listener to be drawn into a small foretaste of the worship of heaven.

What to listen out for in the music in Part III Scene 4

53. Chorus: *'Worthy is the Lamb that was slain'*

The key of this movement is D major, the key ideally suited to the trumpets, which once again join in this final item together with the timpani.

Both parts of the chorus, *'Worthy is the Lamb'* and the 'Amen' chorus, combine block chord and contrapuntal styles in the same way we have met in earlier choruses.

One striking feature is the dignified, majestic opening section (*'Worthy is the Lamb'* through to *'glory and blessing'*), which alternates twice between *largo* and *andante*. But the second *largo andante* is not identical with the first – thus enhancing the musical interest.

In the 'Amen' chorus, in *allegro moderato tempo*, the 'Amen' begins simply in the bass line and continuo with an intricate melody that rises a whole octave within four bars. Each other voice, in ascending order (in other words, bass, tenor, contralto, soprano), also sings the theme once with the other voices providing vocal accompaniment. Somewhat unexpectedly, a solo violin then plays the theme, first on its own and then joined by a *continuo* entrance of the theme, which is interrupted by a choral four-part setting with the theme in the bass. Eventually, after further contrapuntal development, the chorus – and the whole oratorio – end with one last 'Handelian hiatus' before the final *'Amen'*.

A contemporary critic described the fugue on *'Amen'* as 'absurd and without reason'.[2] However, Handel's first biographer, John Mainwaring, wrote in 1760 that this conclusion revealed the composer 'rising still higher' than in 'that vast effort of genius, the Hallelujah Chorus.'[3]

---

[2] Referred to by S. Heighes, 'George Frideric Handel (1685-1759)/Simon Heighes for The Sixteen recording, Ach, Herr, mich armen Sünder' (http://www.hyperion-records.co.uk).

[3] R. Luckett, *'Handel's Messiah: A Celebration'* (London: Victor Gollancz, 1992).

Conclusion

More than entertainment

On one occasion when *Messiah* was performed, Lord Kinnoul complimented Handel on 'a splendid entertainment', but Handel replied, 'My Lord, I should be sorry if I only entertained them; I wished to make them better.'[1]

So, having reached the end of our journey through this outstanding oratorio, how should we respond? The answer must be to take to heart the message that has been communicated by the words and music of *Messiah.* In order to do that, we need to exercise what might best be described as 'bifocal' vision in our approach to the message – in other words to look simultaneously in two directions.

Focus on the Messiah

The first direction in which we need to look is at the Messiah himself, Jesus Christ, the one whose person and work have been the subject matter of the oratorio.

A pivotal incident (referred to in the Introduction) is recorded in each of the first three Gospels, when Jesus asks his disciples two questions (Matt 16:13–16; Mark 8:27–29; Luke 9:18–20).

The first question is: 'Who do people say that I am?' Various answers are given: John the Baptist, Elijah, or one of the prophets. As complimentary and impressive as each of these answers is from people in general, none of them is adequate. They see Jesus as a preparatory figure rather than the fulfilment. For them he belongs to the Old Testament order of things. Many people today who are asked the same question may well give thoughtful and respectful answers, describing Jesus as a good man, an

[1] James Beattie, 'Letter of May 25, 1780' published in W. Forbes, *An Account of the Life and Writings of James Beattie, LL.D.* (1806), 331.

idealist, a great teacher, a miracle-worker and much else besides – but falling short of the true answer.

The second question that Jesus asked his disciples on that significant occasion is: 'But who do you say that I am?' Peter's response in Mark's account is: 'You are the Christ' (Mark 8:29). Peter, on behalf of all the disciples, recognises Jesus as the Christ, the Messiah, the one who fulfils all the promises and expectations of Old Testament Scripture, the one who is God himself who has come to visit and redeem his people (see Luke 1:68). In the words of John the Baptist on a different occasion, Jesus is 'the one who is to come' (Matt 11:3). Jesus accepts Peter's answer as the right one.

Handel's great oratorio, incorporating Jennens's skilfully compiled libretto, unpacks the implications of what Jesus' Messiahship signifies. As we look back over the oratorio, we have seen that Jesus the Messiah is:

- the rescuer (Movements 2–4)
- the judge (Movements 5–6) – although, as we have seen, his role as judge properly belongs to his second coming
- God in person (explicitly in Movement 8 and 12, and implicitly in many others)
- the light of the world (Movements 10–11)
- the healer of mankind's deepest needs (Movement 19)
- the good shepherd (Movement 20)
- the teacher (Movement 20)
- the Lamb of God who takes away the sin of the world by his sacrificial, substitutionary death (Movements 22–30)
- the King of glory (Movement 33)
- the Son (Movement 35)
- the ruler of the nations (Movements 40–44)
- the destroyer of death and the giver of life (Movements 45–50)

- the Lamb upon the throne who is worthy of all honour and glory (Movement 53)

How should we respond to these great truths? If, at the end of a performance of *Messiah,* we simply feel emotionally uplifted and nothing more, we shall have failed to respond to the Messiah who has been presented to us. Who he is and what he has done must impact our lives. In the words of C T Studd, who gave up a life of wealth and sporting fame in order to give himself to overseas missionary service, 'When I came to see that Jesus Christ had died for me, it didn't seem hard to give up all for him. It seemed just common, ordinary honesty.'[2]

Focus on ourselves

The second direction in which we need to look is at ourselves. Serious soul-searching is called for. Not only does *Messiah* direct us to look upwards at the Lord who died and rose and reigns over all, but we are compelled also to look inwards at our own hearts. For this oratorio tells the story of the human race and of each human being individually. Of the many themes contained within the text of the oratorio, we examine briefly just three.

First, the theme of **our exile**. There is a real sense in which that Babylonian exile with which the work began is a representation of the natural condition of mankind, and not just the experience of the people of Judah of the sixth century BC. We noted earlier (in the discussion of Movement 2) that the exile really began in Genesis 3, when the first man and woman were expelled from the Garden where they had enjoyed unbroken fellowship with God. And that has been the natural condition of every human being ever since.

C S Lewis wrote these words about that sense of exile that many experience but without necessarily being able to express it so articulately: 'If I find in myself a desire which no experience in this world can satisfy, the most probable explanation is that I was made for another world.'[3] The next comment, by Jean-Paul Sartre, intended as a statement of unbelief, seems to bear witness to such a 'desire' or deep longing for a way out of

---

[2] Cited in G. Bridger, *The Man from Outside* (Leicester: Inter-Varsity Press, 1978), 193.
[3] C. S. Lewis, *Mere Christianity* (London: Collins/Fontana, 1955), 118.

a sense of exile: 'God is silent and that I cannot deny – everything in me calls for God and that I cannot forget.'[4]

From birth, we are 'in Adam', and without a personal experience of Christ's saving work we are still far from God – 'alienated and hostile in mind' (Col 1:21). The reconciliation, available to us, which the very next verse of Paul's letter tells us about, has been made possible 'in his body of flesh by his death' (Col 1:22). In other words, the true end of the exile was not achieved by King Cyrus's decree in 539 or 538 BC, but it was achieved by the Messiah, Jesus Christ, who died for us and by his Spirit brings about a change of relationship with God for Christian believers, so that we can truly call him 'Abba! Father!' (Gal 4:6).

Second, the theme of **our sinfulness**. The need for sins to be forgiven has been a recurring theme throughout the oratorio. The very first vocal item (Movement 2), with its announcement to Jerusalem that *'her iniquity is pardoned'* (Isa 40:2), is not only a message of *'comfort'* but also a statement that there are sins that need to be forgiven. The reality of judgement has been made plain, for example in Movement 6 (Mal 3:2: *'But who may abide the day of his coming?'*). Here are truths for all of us to face up to. Even if we would prefer not to do this, we nevertheless find it difficult to disagree with Mark Twain when he said, 'Man is the only animal that blushes. Or needs to.'[5] The text of *Messiah* makes effective use of the Bible's picture of darkness to illustrate the natural condition of mankind. This comes particularly in the texts from Isaiah in Part I Scene 3. In Part II of the oratorio we are invited to recognise ourselves included in the 'we' of Isaiah 53:4–6 as those who acknowledge, *'All we like sheep have gone astray'* (Movement 26) and as those who recognise, *'Surely he hath borne **our** griefs and carried **our** sorrows'* (my emphasis) (Movement 24).

And alongside the recurring theme of human sinfulness (our sinfulness), we find ourselves encouraged to respond with amazement to the good news that Jesus is *'the Lamb of God that taketh away the sins of the world'* (John 1:29, Movement 22) and that *'the Lord hath laid on him the iniquity of us all'* (Isa 53:6, Movement 26).

[4] Cited in C.I. Glicksberg, *Literature and Religion* (Dallas: Southern Methodist University Press, 1960), 221–22.

[5] M. Twain, *Following the Equator* (Hartford: American Publishing Company, 1897).

Third, the theme of **our mortality**. As was discussed earlier, the theme of death is not a popular topic of conversation. We may well feel that Woody Allen got it right when he said, 'I am not afraid of death, I just don't want to be there when it happens.'[6] But in our more honest moments, we know that such a wish cannot be granted – unless Christ's second coming comes first. To quote George Bernard Shaw, 'Death is the ultimate statistic – one out of one will die.'[7] Handel's *Messiah,* particularly Part III, encourages us to face up to that truth but it also opens up for us the only answer to the reality of human mortality: *'For as in Adam all die, even so in Christ shall all be made alive'* (1 Cor 15:22, Movement 46). The whole of mankind is included in the first 'all', for all are born 'in Adam.' The second 'all' are those who know that by God's grace they are 'in Christ.'

Here, then, are three themes from Handel's oratorio (our own natural condition of exile or alienation, our own sinfulness, and our own mortality) which should help us in the second part of our 'bifocal' exercise to look at our own individual personal need of what only Jesus Christ, the Messiah, can fulfil.

Responding to the Messiah

Every performance of *Messiah* is a declaration of the gospel, and the oratorio delivers a challenge to all who hear it – both through the work as a whole and also through what was described earlier as the 'evangelistic appeal' of the end of Part I.

It could be that you, as a reader of this book, realise that you have never before faced up to the real Jesus Christ who has been so clearly introduced to us through Handel's *Messiah* from the Bible record. If that is you, may I invite you to consider Jesus and your need of him in the light of eternity? Please do not dismiss the following words quoted from J C Ryle, the first Bishop of Liverpool, as 'over the top' – but rather see them as thoroughly consistent with the message of *Messiah* both in their warning and in their invitation:

> I tell you that at this moment there are only two places in which your sins can be, and I defy the wisdom of

[6] Cited in D. C. K. Watson, *Is Anyone There?* (London: Hodder and Stoughton, 1979), 64.
[7] Cited in D. C. K. Watson, *In Search of God* (London: Falcon, 1974), 80.

> the world to find out a third. Either your sins are UPON YOURSELF, unpardoned, unforgiven, uncleansed, unwashed away – sinking you daily nearer to hell! Or else your sins are UPON CHRIST, taken away, forgiven, pardoned, blotted out and cleansed away by Christ's precious blood! I am utterly unable to see any third place in which a man's sins can possibly be. I am utterly unable to discover any third alternative. Forgiven or unforgiven – pardoned or not pardoned; cleansed away or not cleansed – this, according to the Bible, is the exact position of everyone's sins. How is it with you? 'Where are your sins?'[8]

This was exactly the realisation that struck Charles Simeon with such forcefulness and led him to trust Jesus as Saviour. The account of his conversion was included in the discussion on Movement 22. We considered earlier on, in the discussion of Movement 20, Jesus' own invitation to those who recognise that they are bearing a heavy burden of sin – he says, 'Come to me, all who labour and are heavy laden, and I will give you rest' (Matt 11:28).

The Bible's instructions, at their very simplest, on how to get right with God are to repent and believe. Jesus' first recorded words in Mark's Gospel are: 'The time is fulfilled, and the kingdom of God is at hand; repent and believe in the gospel' (Mark 1:15). We are given here two truths and two commands:

- Truth 1: the time of preparation is over, because Jesus has come as the fulfilment of all the promises of the coming Messiah.
- Truth 2: he is the King, which is what is implied by the 'kingdom of God' being at hand, and therefore he has come with all authority.
- Command 1: he calls on people to repent – to turn from their sins and recognise their need of forgiveness.

[8] J.C. Ryle, *Old Paths* (London: William Hunt and Company, 1895), 174.

- Command 2: he calls on people to believe the gospel – and the 'good news' (which is what 'gospel' means) is that he is the Saviour we need who provides that forgiveness.

If you have already put your trust in Christ, may I encourage you to do three things?

- to *know* this Messiah more and more. We can do that chiefly through the Bible. Daily Bible reading is to be recommended: just a short passage, perhaps with the help of Bible reading notes.[9] Coupling our daily Bible reading with prayer is a good idea – in other words, talking back to God about the things he has been speaking to you in your Bible reading. Getting involved in a church where the Bible is faithfully taught and where you find the encouragement of Christian friends is helpful too.

- to *love* this Messiah more and more. This phrase is not to be understood in any sentimental way but is the best description of a growing personal relationship with the one who 'first loved us' (1 John 4:19). Growth in the Christian life begins with the mind, as we take on board the truths of Bible teaching, but it is not meant to remain head-knowledge only. It must warm our hearts and energise our wills. Christians of an earlier generation used to talk regularly of our 'affections' – in other words, the desires and inclinations of our whole person. And here too Christ must be Lord.

- to *serve* this Messiah more and more. We do this by obeying him and honouring him as Lord in our daily lives – putting him first in everything in the home and family, in the workplace, in leisure time. There may be specific Christian work you can take on in your church, and many believers have found that active involvement in Christian service has been a real source of encouragement and Christian growth.

This threefold growth in Christian discipleship is expressed well in an old prayer by Richard of Chichester:

---

[9] Such as 'Explore', published by the Good Book Company.

Thanks be to thee, our Lord Jesus Christ,
for all the benefits which thou hast given us,
for all the pains and insults which thou hast borne for us.
O most merciful Redeemer, Friend and Brother,
may we know thee more clearly,
love thee more dearly,
and follow thee more nearly,
now and for ever.[10]

Worthy is the Lamb

The most appropriate ending is to return to the final scene of *Messiah* and join in the chorus of praise and worship around the throne. Here then, in the ESV version of parts of Revelation 5:9–10 and 12–14, are the words of the 'new song' of the four living creatures and the twenty-four elders, followed by the loud shout of praise of myriads of myriads and thousands of thousands of angels, and then the praise of every creature in heaven and on the earth and under the earth and in the sea:

Worthy are you to take the scroll and to open its seals,
for you were slain, and by your blood you ransomed people for God
from every tribe and language and people and nation,
and you have made them a kingdom and priests to our God,
and they shall reign on the earth.

Worthy is the Lamb who was slain,
to receive power and wealth and wisdom and might
and honour and glory and blessing!

To him who sits upon the throne and to the Lamb
be blessing and honour and glory and might for ever and ever.

Amen!

[10] F. Colquhoun, *Family Prayers* (London: SPCK/Triangle, 1987), 62.

Appendix 1: Charles Jennens's original titles for the libretto of *Messiah*

Part I: The prophecy and realisation of God's plan to redeem mankind by the coming of the Messiah
Scene 1: Isaiah's prophecy of salvation (Movements 1–4)
Scene 2: The prophecy of the coming of Messiah and the question, despite (1), of what this may portend for the World (Movements 5–7)
Scene 3: The prophecy of the Virgin Birth (Movements 8–12)
Scene 4: The appearance of the Angels to the Shepherds (Movements 13–17)
Scene 5: Christ's redemptive miracles on earth (Movements 18–21)

Part II: The accomplishment of redemption by the sacrifice of Christ, mankind's rejection of God's offer, and mankind's utter defeat when trying to oppose the power of the Almighty
Scene 1: The redemptive sacrifice, the scourging and the agony on the cross (Movements 22–30)
Scene 2: His sacrificial death, His passage through Hell and resurrection (Movements 31–32)
Scene 3: His ascension (Movement 33)
Scene 4: God discloses His identity in Heaven (Movements 34–35)
Scene 5: Whitsun, the gift of tongues, the beginning of evangelism (Movements 36–39)
Scene 6: The world and its rulers reject the Gospel (Movements 40–42)
Scene 7: God's triumph (Movements 43–44)

Part III: A Hymn of Thanksgiving for the final overthrow of Death
Scene 1: The promise of bodily resurrection and redemption from Adam's fall (Movements 45–46)
Scene 2: The Day of Judgement and general resurrection (Movements 47–48)
Scene 3: The victory over death and sin (Movements 49–52)
Scene 4: The glorification of the Messianic victim (Movement 53)

Appendix 2: A table of dates in biblical history

This chronological table includes events that are referred to in the course of the book, mostly in Part I, plus a few others. Names of prophets are in italics.

BC

2000 (approx)	God promises Abraham a land and a people – and that through him all nations of the earth will be blessed (Gen 12:1–3)
1000 (approx)	God promises David that he will raise up the offspring of David and establish the throne of his kingdom for ever (2 Sam 7:12–13)
735	Ahaz, king of Judah, is faced with the threat from Israel and Syria, and *Isaiah* gives him the promise of the virgin's son (Isa 7)
722	Fall of Samaria, capital of the northern kingdom of Israel, and the population of Israel deported to Assyria (2 Kings 17)
712	Visit to Hezekiah, king of Judah, by ambassadors from Merodach-Baladan, king of Babylon (Isa 39)
605	Daniel and a select few are deported to Babylon (Dan 1:1–7)
597	The first main captivity of the people of Judah. Jehoiachin (the king), the skilled men and the temple treasures are deported to Babylon (2 Kings 24:12–16)
587	Fall of Jerusalem to the Babylonians and second stage of captivity (Jer 39)
582/1	A third deportation to Babylon
539/8	Cyrus, king of Persia, liberates the captives (Ezra 1:1–4)
520	*Haggai* prophesies while Zerubbabel is governor of Judah and Joshua is high priest; *Zechariah* also prophesies around this time
c.517	Letter of Darius I to Tattenai, governor of the province Beyond the River, instructing him to provide various material help in the rebuilding of the temple (Ezra 5:6–17)
c.460	*Malachi* prophesies in Judah

? 8/7	Birth of Jesus Christ, the Messiah
AD	
33	Jesus' triumphal entry into Jerusalem; crucifixion and resurrection; Pentecost
49	Council of Jerusalem
70	Fall of Jerusalem to the Romans

Appendix 3: Musical terms

a cappella: literally "in the church style," and is therefore applied to unaccompanied vocal music.

accompagnato: similar to "recitative" – but see "recitative" below for an explanation of the difference.

adagio: slow.

air (or aria): a solo vocal piece of melodious character.

allegro: quick, lively.

alto: see "contralto."

arioso: a short but aria-like, sustained, developed, dignified vocal piece.

Baroque: when applied to music, this term refers to the distinctive musical style of the late 17th and early 18th centuries.

bass: the lowest of the male voices.

binary form: the pattern of a piece of music consisting of two parts of more or less equal length, often with the first half starting in the home key and modulating into a related key and with the second half finally returning to the home key.

block chord: the style of harmonic progression, in which the four vocal lines sing the same words in the same metre and rhythm as each other, as when a church-choir sings a hymn or as in a Bach chorale. Also known as "homophony."

bridge passage: a section of music which links two distinct sections of a piece of music, often by means of modulation bringing about a change of tonality (or key).

cantus firmus: a fixed melody to which other voices are added.

chorale: see "block chord" above.

chorus: a piece within the oratorio for the four-part choir to sing, rather than a soloist.

chromatic: introducing notes not forming a part of the prevailing key. A chromatic scale progresses by semitones.

coloratura: the extemporary or written decoration of a vocal melody in the shape of runs and similar embellishments.

continuo: an independent bass line, usually realized on a keyboard instrument, in which numerals written underneath the notes indicate the kinds of harmony to be played.

contralto: the lowest of the female voices. The shortened form "alto" is normally used for males with this pitch of voice.

counterpoint (adjectival form: "contrapuntal"): a feature of composition, where one part enters with a phrase, which is then more or less exactly copied by other parts in succession while the earlier part(s) is/are still playing (or singing). Also known as "polyphony."

countersubject: this term is used in connection with a fugue and refers to the theme in one voice that accompanies the statement of the original subject in another voice.

counter-tenor: male alto.

crotchet: a musical note which represents the normal "pulse" of a piece, its time-value being half that of a minim.

da capo: literally "from the head," the term means "Go back to the beginning, start again, and continue until you come to the word Fine ('End')." Often abbreviated to "D.C."

diminuendo: gradually getting softer in volume.

dotted rhythm: repeated sequence of a dotted note (i.e. lengthened by half) followed by a note which has half the normal value.

duet: a piece of music for two vocalists or instrumentalists, with or without accompaniment.

fifth: see "interval."

forte: loud.

fourth: see "interval." An "augmented" fourth is one semitone more than a fourth.

fugue: a piece with sustained use of counterpoint (see above).

grave: with slow speed and solemnity.

harmony: the combination of different notes, or lines of notes, by vocalists or instrumentalists. Depending on the context, it can be the opposite of "unison" (see below) or "discord."

home key: the tonality of the piece of music, as indicated by its key-signature. It is the key in which the piece would normally be expected to begin and finish.

homophony: see "block chord."

interval: the difference of pitch between two notes of the scale, measured by counting inclusively between them, e.g. C to E is a "third."

key: refers to the adherence in a piece of music to the note-material of one of the major or minor scales – see "minor" below.

largo: literally "broad," and therefore means slow and dignified.

libretto: the Italian word for "little book," meaning the literary text of an opera or oratorio.

melisma: a term used of passages in which one syllable flowers out into a passage of several notes.

mezzo-soprano: the female voice between soprano and contralto.

minor: best explained by contrast to its opposite, which is "major." The scale of C major consists of the white notes on a piano keyboard: C-D-E-F-G-A-B-C. The scale of C minor in its so-called "harmonic" form consists of the notes: C-D-Eb-F-G-Ab-B-C. A minor key sounds more mournful than a major key.

modulate: change key within the course of a passage.

movement: a distinct major section within a larger piece of music, such as a symphony or concerto. In this study the term is applied to the separate items within the oratorio.

obbligato: when attached to the “part” of any instrument in a score, the implication is that the part in question is essential to the effect.

octave: the interval between one note and another which is eight steps above it or below it, counting inclusively – i.e. when ascending, or descending, the scale from that first note by eight steps (counting inclusively). Two notes an octave apart, played or sung together, have a hollow-sounding quality.

oratorio: an extended setting of a religious libretto for solo vocalists, chorus and orchestra, and designed for either a concert or church performance, i.e. without scenery, costume or action.

overture: in Handel’s time the word meant a piece of instrumental music intended as the introduction to an oratorio or an opera (the word “symphony” was also used).

piano: soft.

Pifa: an alternative name for the “Pastoral Symphony,” one of the movements in this oratorio.

postlude: the converse of “prelude,” normally referring to the concluding part of a piece played by the orchestra after the end of the soloist’s air.

prestissimo: very fast.

quaver: a musical note with the time-value of one-half of a crotchet (and one-eighth the time-value of a semi-breve, which is the whole note).

recitative: a style of solo vocal composition in which ordered melody, rhythm and metre are largely disregarded in favour of some imitation of the natural inflections of speech and accompanied by only the continuo (in contrast to items marked “accompagnato,” which are accompanied by additional string instruments).

second: see “interval.”

semiquaver: a musical note with the time-value of one-half of a quaver.

semitone: the smallest interval used in normal music, as for example between the notes B and C.

soprano: the highest of the female voices, above mezzo-soprano and contralto.

symphony: in Handel's use of the term, it means an introducing, closing, or interpolated instrumental passage within the oratorio, such as the "Pastoral Symphony" in Part I.

tempo: speed.

tenor: the male voice that is next in height above a bass and a baritone, but lower than counter-tenor.

ternary form: the shape of a piece of music that falls into three parts, with the third part being essentially a repeat of the first – i.e. the shape is A-B-A.

third: see "interval."

time signature: the composer's indication in the score of the metre of the piece of music.

timpani: the Italian word for kettle-drums.

tonic sol-fa: a system of singing, in which – irrespective of the musical key – each note is designated according to its position in that key. So, when going through the key of C from an initial C to the C which is one octave higher, the notes are labelled "do," "re," "mi," "fa," "so," "la," "te" and "do." As a footnote in this book comments, the famous song "Do-Re-Mi" from "The Sound of Music" provides a helpful explanation.

unison: a line of music provided by more than one vocalist or instrumentalist, all singing or playing exactly the same notes.

Recently Released by the Latimer Trust

Come, Let Us Sing: A Call to Musical Reformation by Robert S. Smith

Come, Let Us Sing seeks to help us reform the musical dimension of church life by bringing biblical clarity to two key questions: Why do we come together? and Why do we sing together?

In answer to the first, Robert Smith navigates a path through the contemporary 'worship word wars', concluding that we gather both to worship God and to encourage others. Two questions must, therefore, be asked of everything we do: Does it glorify God? and Does it edify others?

As to why we sing, Smith unpacks three principal functions of congregational singing in Scripture – as a way of praising, a way of praying and a way of preaching. In so doing, he explores the necessity of singing scriptural truth, the value of psalmody, the place of emotions, the role of our bodies, and how singing expresses and enriches our unity.
Come, Let Us Sing is a timely call for the church to reclaim its biblical musical heritage and reform its musical practice.

The Anglican Ordinal. Gospel Priorities for Church of England Ministry by Andrew Atherstone

This book is part of our *Anglican Foundation* series, which offer practical guidance on Church of England services.

There is no better handbook for Anglican ministry than the Anglican ordinal – the authorized liturgy for ordaining new ministers. The ordinal contains a beautiful, succinct description of theological priorities and ministry models for today's Church. This booklet offers a simple exposition of the ordinal's primary themes. Anglican clergy are called to public ministry as messengers, sentinels, stewards, and shepherds. They are asked searching questions and they make solemn promises. The Holy Spirit's anointing is invoked upon their ministries, with the laying-on-of-hands, and they are gifted a Bible as the visual symbol of their new pastoral and preaching office. This booklet is a handy primer for ordinands and clergy, and all those responsible for their selection, training, and deployment.

Also in the Latimer Studies' series:

Synods by Gerald Bray

Synods are gatherings of church officers that convene for the purpose of deliberating what church policy should be. Their agenda may include resolving disputes that have arisen as well, as making plans for the future development of the life of the church.

They are typically representative bodies, though who they represent varies from time to time and from church to church. They have been held from the very earliest days of Christianity, and for many centuries they were understood to be assemblies of bishops. That is still the case in the Roman Catholic and Eastern Orthodox churches, but Anglican practice is much broader in scope, including clergy and laity as well. Modern synods also meet on a regular basis and operate according to a fixed constitution. They share some features in common with those of other times and places, but they are not direct descendants of any particular ancient tradition. There is no form of Anglican synodical government beyond the level of the national church, a fact that has become increasingly problematic in the worldwide Anglican Communion. Reform of the national synodical structure and the development of an effective form of synodical government that will be regarded as authoritative by the entire Communion are the greatest challenges we face today and it is these that this essay seeks to address.

Lex Orandi, Lex Credendi by Martin Davie

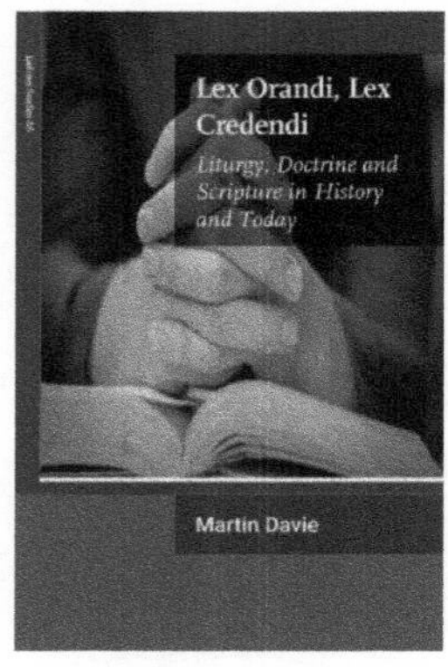

The Latin phrase *lex orandi, lex credendi* ('the law of praying is the law of believing') is a phrase which is often used in Anglican theological discussion, but which needs careful unpacking if its meaning is to be properly understood.

In this study Martin Davie provides such unpacking. He traces the history of the phrase back to its origins in the work of St. Prosper of Aquitaine in the fifth century, explains what it means and gives examples of how it has been both used and misused in the Roman Catholic, Orthodox and Anglican traditions.

His conclusion is that when it is rightly understood the principle *lex orandi, lex credendi* provides a useful tool for assessing both a church's liturgy and its doctrine. It reminds us that a church's liturgical practice needs to cohere with its doctrine and both need to be in line with Scripture.

He also argues that the use of this tool shows us that not only are proposals for marking same-sex relationships unacceptable, but so also is the new proposal to use liturgy to mark gender transition.

Lightning Source UK Ltd.
Milton Keynes UK
UKHW011956200221
378988UK00001B/24